DAILIES

Day-To-Day
Reminders
from My Spirit Guides

by
C. A. Filius

Copyright © 2011 Charles A. Filius

ISBN 13: 978-0-615-58076-0

All Rights Reserved. No part of this book may be reproduced, stored in a retrieval system, or transmitted in any form, by any means, including mechanical, electric, photocopying, recording or otherwise, without the prior written permission of the publisher and author.

Inquiries: P O Box 27624 • Anaheim, CA 92809

Printed in the United State of America

Acknowledgements

Travis Ayers, Mike Berry, Mona Masonis-Boyer,
Tim Braun, John & Rose Culbertson,
Chris & Dawn Carroll DeMint, Suzie Estridge, Ed Hicks,
Robbi Hutton, Angela Laguardia, Rebeka Lopez, Barb Mallon,
Craig Massey, Thomas Moore, Robert Nelson, Nicole Noles,
James W. Powell, Donna Repp, Kaie Rudolph,
Aaron J. Shelton, Gregg & Darlene Spaete, Darleen Summers,
Robert Tinnell, Anthony Vingas,
Everyone at The Factory in Monessen…

and

♥ Ruth R. Powell ♥
You've added so much beauty to my life, Aunt Ruth.
Thank you.

For Margo

You are far too young to be so old.

Your voice brought me back to mine.
I am forever grateful.

"The way I see it,
it doesn't matter what you believe
just so you're sincere."

~ *Linus van Pelt*

"THE SIGNPOST UP AHEAD"

"Nature does not hurry, yet everything is accomplished."
– Lao Tzu

I OFTEN ASK MYSELF WHY I ENDED UP HERE. Why *here*? Why did I end up with this particular life, this set of circumstances and the parties directly, and indirectly, involved?

I remember as a kid watching a sequence in one of the masterful 'Charlie Brown' cartoons where he and Linus are walking along the beach. Charlie Brown innocently picks up a stone and tosses it out into the sea. Linus immediately chastises him for it, saying that it had taken that pebble centuries to finally make it out of the water and now it has to start its journey all over again. Boy, I wanted to punch Linus. But then I started to think about that moment. Was Charlie Brown destined to toss that pebble into the sea? Or was that his free will? What put Charlie Brown in that scenario at that moment is exactly what put me here: a skilled artisan with a twisted three-bricks-shy-of-a-full-load sense of humor.

It tends to bewilder me, on an hourly basis, just how I got here. What am I supposed to be learning? More importantly, why am I supposed to be learning it? I spent the first forty years of my life convinced that life was nothing more than a onetime free-for-all; no rhyme, reason or rules worth repeating. Of course, as I often am, I was wrong. (In the words of the great philosopher, Gomer Pyle, *"Surprise! Surprise! Surprise!"*)

Dailies

The navigation along any pathway requires a map, just ask anyone from the local auto club—or NASA. The same goes with the journey on the road of life. You can obsessively construct a detailed syllabus to get through your daily travels, or you can wing it, living in a state of denial and allowing yourself to believe you're on your own. It doesn't matter—just as long as you actually do something! Steps must be taken, in some form, in order to move onward and upward. If you just sit in your recliner lamenting on what could be and should be you're only going to get soft in the middle and have your ass-print saved for posterity.

We're pretty much spoon-fed the idealistic goals of the life ahead of us from day one. The collective brass rings—education, family, home, career—weigh down our wrists and can, at times, slow us down. We are conditioned to seek out these ambitions and aspirations. Or, perhaps, you boldly decide to take a different path. You opt to open yourself up to larger things, taking yourself to greater heights by letting the light of your Higher Self chart your course. Be warned, though, this light, this amazingly bright light, tends to alter your original perspective. I am speaking from personal experience, folks. My origins pushed me in one direction on a gravel back road until my destiny grabbed me by the collar and jerked me into the freeway HOV lane. It's like a spiritual funhouse mirror, distorting your perception just enough for you to realize that things don't look quite right. But that image isn't a funny one because, whereas you thought you were headed down the right road to get to a particular point, you find that you were meant to go in an entirely different direction. Suddenly all of those goals that fueled you are now lackluster and dull. And you find yourself once again scratching your noggin as you squint, trying to get a sharper view of that signpost up ahead. It's the equivalent of uttering, "I knew I should have made that left turn at Albuquerque!" Until now I bet you never thought of

Day-To-Day Reminders

Dailies

Bugs Bunny as being spiritually aware. Or would that be spiritually '*a-hare*'? Hey, don't blame me. One of my guides wrote that and it *will* be taken out of his paycheck.

You've just witnessed history in the making, folks. I have officially passed the buck to the other side.

But where do you go for directions? This ultra-electronic age provides us with a vast multitude of options—each one more void of human interaction than the one before it—to send us on our merry way. From Internet search engines to the GPS in your car to the latest must-have app for your upgraded *iWhatChaMaDiggerThingy*. There are always choices for some form of directional input. There was a time when certain individuals would be happy to tell you where to go, now inanimate objects are doing it. It's only a matter of time before blenders turn on us and flip everyone off.

Instead of technology, which gets us nowhere, you can always seek out God, The Great Spirit, The Man Upstairs—whatever term you prefer—for Guidance. Lord knows the insight is available. How we perceive and interpret it is up to us, and no, there isn't an app for the smarter-than-you phone to help us figure it out. Plugging into our own Spirit Guides and Angels is another scenic route to take along the Transcendental Highway. This is the route I've taken, and lucky for me, I have a set of Guides that would make any Route 66 tourist green with envy.

* * *

Other than the puzzled inquiries regarding my Rubik's Cube-like fashion sense, the most common questions I receive from clients these days relate to my Spirit Guides.

Day-To-Day Reminders

Dailies _____

    A) "Who are they?"

    B) "What do they do?"

    C) "Why are they with you?"

    D) "What's their purpose?"

The answers are:

    A) The names they've given to me are Robert, Laura, Martin, Christopher, Pamela, Oliver, The One Who Soars with Eagles, Dondi, Thomas, and Joseph. Of course, the names mean nothing to them. They gave them to me so *I* feel comfortable about our interactions. They look out for *me*, not the other way around. I don't have an ear for language or dialect; if someone speaks with a heavy accent, he might as well be speaking a foreign language. For me, the subtle nuances of the vernacular blur together like a particularly wet sneeze bombarding a Roger Armstrong watercolor so that there isn't much left behind. It's why I don't listen to much music, I simply can't grasp the lyrics quickly enough to enjoy the song. It's nothing but a jumbled racket. So it makes sense that my guides would use rather simplistic names. The lone exception is The One Who Soars with Eagles, my Guide who comes to me in the form of a Native American. When he first told me what to call him, I knew immediately that it wasn't his true name. It sounds oh-so-stereotypically contrived, right? So I called him on it and asked him for his real name. His response was, like all of his communication with me, direct and to the point. With absolute certainty, he stated, "You would not be able to pronounce it if I told you." Makes sense to me.

B) They pass on information and insight to me. These tidbits, which I am sharing with you in this book, are beneficial to me on a singular level, but the benefits I received from their knowledge extend outward from me and encompass a larger realm. My Guides assist me with my readings, my writings, my drawing, and my day-to-day routines. And I in turn share their insights with others in the hopes of helping those who find me.

C) They clearly lost a bet with God.

D) They shed light on love and life everlasting. They prove truth to the heart that the mind can never grasp. The ways in which they make themselves known is as infinite as the heavens. Sometimes I'm aware, but in most cases, I'm oblivious. For me, that's the best way to go about it. If I ever become aware, there's an excellent chance of a major faux pas descending upon me like crazed shoppers on Black Friday bombarding the aisles in search of the 99-cent waffle iron. In other words, they work in the background so I won't look so bad. Even with the current staff of ten they are horribly shorthanded. Or so Robert, my Master Guide, continually tells me.

***

Just like you and me, each of my Spirit Guides has very distinctive personalities. And why not? They were once here in the physical world. They've gone through all of this and literally lived to tell the tale. While we meander through the corridors in P.S. Earth, they've already transferred to a better school. They're not perfect. They're the first to tell me that. They're still learning, expanding, evolving, being. They do have a slight upper hand by being more aware of this fact than I am. They have rules and regulations—they're not allowed to reveal too much to me. I have to learn, not recite. Most importantly, they will never, under any circumstance, tell me what to do. They're here to offer guidance. Hence the name: 'Guide.' If they were supposed to tell me what to do, they would be called 'Mom.'

Some believe that each of us has only one Spirit Guide. Other spirits who enter our playground are merely "spirit helpers." I have to disrespectfully disagree. I have, as of this writing, ten. Of course, I'm quite difficult, so it makes sense that they have to pull out the big guns to get me under some illusion of control.

* * *

My experience with my Etheric Entourage has been a stellar teaching tool. They are right there, step by step, thought by thought, as I meander through my own maze in search of the celestial cheese. Some refer to the daily assistance from their own spirit guides as "intuition" or "that little voice in my head." When I first began communicating with them, on the other hand, I considered it "schizophrenia." Try interacting with ten Guides and you'll know what I mean.

Luckily for us, you don't have to be aware of their interaction within your own life, let alone of their existence, to benefit from their unique hands-on approach. Unlike mere mortals, they do not look for accolades or a plaque proclaiming them Employee of the Month. There's a lesson in humility to be learned here, but let's face it, the human side of us enjoys a good pat on the back every now and again. For me, sharing the lessons from my Crew is my way of giving them that "Atta-boy!" and that pat on the head.

If they even have heads.

* * *

So this brings me back to my earlier question: Where do you go for direction? All you really need to do is be open and aware. Accept the signs that are shown, take the time to find the not-so-obvious ones, and you'll have your map. I'm sure you're a lot like me and you find insight, inspiration and a good old-fashioned poke in the ribs originating within a variety of sources. Some are expected; others not so much. Then there are the ones that really knock you out of your Buster Browns: Those huge slivers of wide-eyed wonderment that come from the most unexpected of places.

I've received a number of those out-of-the-blue messages over the past decade. They've come through allegedly wrong numbers at just the right time, total strangers approaching me with gifts while standing in line at the Multi-Plex, and even finding seemingly random coins in very out-of-the-way places.

For example, in May 2005, I was scheduled for my very first official group mediumship demonstration at a new age bookstore. The owners, both very dear friends of mine, had ~~badgered~~ encouraged me into jumping feet first out of my comfort zone of psychic fairs and phone readings and onto the platform before a mostly live audience. Before I caved to their screaming demands I asked my Spirit Guides for a sign that it was the right time in my own development to do this. I was, admittedly, terrified at the prospect. There's a huge difference between reading one person over the phone and having a

Dailies

whole room fixated on your every word. I was given the choice of two dates for my demo and I immediately had my confirmation. One of the dates would have been my maternal grandparent's 89th wedding anniversary. My grandparents were surrogate parents to me. My mom and I moved in with them when I was less than two years old. While one lone date may not initially seem like a big deal to you, trust me, it really was. And, like each of my spiritual adventures, that was only the beginning.

The day of the event had arrived. As I was walking from my car to the store I passed a pay phone (my younger readers may have to Google that reference). When I was 11-years-old one of my cousins put me in the habit of checking for money left behind in the coin return slot of a pay phone. So, as usual, I checked the coin return and found nothing. I did, however, find a row of pennies along the top of the phone. There were six of them neatly aligned (I am a 'six' in numerology). Five of the coins were tails up. Lincoln's profile stared at me from the sixth. The date of this lone nonconformist cent was 1966, the year of my grandparent's 50th wedding anniversary. I was five years old and I remember the event quite clearly. We had a huge party in the house that seemed to last all day. I had never seen that many people under our roof at any given time. Guests were milling around in a whirlwind of cake and punch, both heavily laden with massive amounts of 1960s sugar, congratulating the couple at their half-century mark. It was a chance for friends and loved ones to come together in joy and celebration.

And here I was, 39 years later, staring at a row of pennies, about to bring together another reunion of friends and loved ones. What really drove the point home to me was that my grandfather hoarded pennies. He had a strange obsession with them, which was never explained to me. He would pull them

Day-To-Day Reminders

out of any spare change he had and put them in a mason jar. When that jar was filled he'd move on to another one and another. Since I wanted to be like my grandfather I, too, started putting pennies in a jar. Pennies from Heaven took on a whole new meaning for me that day.

As far as I was concerned, I had my sign and then some. I scooped up the pennies and embarked on the evening's events with a faithful calm that can best be described as simply 'knowing' all would be as it should be. I acknowledged my grandparent's wedding anniversary to the packed room that night. I even dedicated the demonstration to their loving memory. There's no doubt in my mind that they were both right there with me, beaming as proud grandparents tend to do.

In case you're wondering, yes, I still have the pennies that I found that day, as well as the jars my grandfather and I filled together.

* * *

The most recent earth-shattering moment to get my attention wasn't shouted from somewhere upon High. There was nothing carved in stone. No burning bush or even an electronic recording promising to self-destruct in five seconds (how cool would that be?). This soul-shaker ambushed me in a well-orchestrated sneak attack originating from behind the most brilliant set of turquoise eyes I have ever seen.

* * *

"Nature always finds a way."

Dailies _____

"What?" I said absent-mindedly. I was, as usual, caught up in my own brand of hibernation: listening to totally pointless mind rants that pertained to absolutely nothing going on around me. I was depressed and nothing, not even the beauty of nature, could shake me from my negativity. I like to think I was trying my best to work myself out of my funk but, in reality, I was attempting to phone it in and all the lines were down. I cannot really explain why I was depressed. Sometimes it just comes over me with what I assume is little rhyme or reason. One moment everything is peaches and cream and the next it's more like a pint of cottage cheese well beyond its expiration date.

Margo turned to me, her camera still pointing at a babbling brook that had momentarily captured her attention and her spirit. I didn't see the beauty, of course, I just saw a creek that would've been at home on one of those annoying motivational posters that hang on the office walls of people who really hate their jobs but would never admit it. "Look," she indicated to the front with a slight nod of her head. "Nature always finds a way." She turned back, snapped a photo and continued, "Those trees had to find the sun on their own to survive." Her camera digitally captured yet another moment in time.

We were standing on a tourist pathway winding within the Muir Woods, surrounded by a serene beauty that can best be explained as a ballet frozen in time and space. In the distance before us stood a cluster of tall trees stretching and turning in their own seemingly awkward alignment reaching for the sky, or more specifically, the light. They craved the source of their life from above while being firmly rooted within their physical origins. They defied convention and manipulated their reality into a better one. They took what they had and changed it to what they, and their surroundings, truly needed. There was no disruption, only cooperation.

Day-To-Day Reminders _____

That's what Margo saw anyway. I was too bogged down inside my thoughts to notice the natural beauty around me.

"We can learn a lot from nature," she continued. "All of nature co-exists. Too bad others won't learn it themselves." No doubt about it, hanging out with Margo was like having my own sliver of Haight-Ashbury at my beck and call.

"People don't change," I said. "We keep gushing over all of our progress to feel important but we're basically getting nowhere." I looked down as I started to wander along the tourist-trodden pathway. "We're hopelessly lost but making damn good time."

"Change is simple," she said. Her emphasis was basic in tone but confident enough to move mountains, or in this case, part creeks. I, on the other hand, was an unmovable, unflinching mound of melancholy. "You just do it if you really want to."

I sighed under my breath. "I'm so not in the mood for this today," I thought to myself. Admittedly, at the time I had been overstaying my welcome at an exclusive pity party of my own design. Words were failing me and my hands were incapable of making a single pencil stroke. If my mind were any blanker I would have been accused of being a dry erase board with no marker in sight. I felt that I could not write down a single syllable of substance let alone one of those 'complete sentences' you hear so much about in literary circles. My motivation, as well as enthusiasm, had left me without providing a forwarding address. I felt empty eyes staring through a canvas before me and I didn't have the slightest inclination to pick up a brush.

The most humiliating thing of all was that I didn't seem to care one way or the other. I was a bucket of sunbeams, believe me.

Dailies

Before I could respond, Margo was bolting ahead on the tree-lined trail. "Look at this!" she exclaimed with genuine awe as she pointed a delicate hand at a cropping of trees just ahead. "Isn't that beautiful?"

My eyes followed her extended forefinger (I'm accustomed to other projected fingers but that's another story for another time). She was pointing to a nearly perfect line of majestic trees standing at attention all the way up the hillside. Each tree standing alongside the next, giving the impression that they were standing watch over all who visit there. Each tree seemed more like an assortment of strands of petrified rope intertwined with the others, creating these massive pillars of living history, one after another after another after another. My eyes followed the row as the trees melded into deeper foliage near the top of the hill. "Yea," I said. "Beautiful." I saw the beauty, but didn't feel it. I knew I should've been feeling something, but in my state, I felt nothing. I was forcing myself to go through the motions but getting nowhere, much like a dog chasing its tail.

It didn't really matter anyway as Margo hadn't heard a word I said. She was already going off road, scurrying up the hillside like an excited kid hopped up on sugar. Dirt and debris flew out from under her shoes with such velocity that anyone directly behind her would have greatly benefited from safety goggles. When her feet didn't provide quite enough traction, she had no problem digging her hands into the soil in front of her. She pulled herself along the way grabbing what she could. Rocks, roots and weeds, it was as if they were there solely to help her on her way. She slid a little here and there but it was evident she was going to get where she wanted to go with no questions asked. I know her well enough to recognize she does not take 'no' as an acceptable answer. A hurricane might one

Day-To-Day Reminders

Dailies

day be named after her but it won't live up to its namesake's determination.

"Do you need some help?" I asked mostly for my own entertainment.

"Why would I want that?" she laughed as she triumphantly pulled herself into the comforting curve shared between two neighboring trees. She crawled between them gracefully, naturally. She sat, pulling her knees up against her chest as if curling up on the lap of some great, unseen Santa. She smiled. She aimed her turquoise eyes at me and shot me a look of contentment, of self-satisfaction, of accomplishment.

Now the landscape was truly beautiful. Not because Margo was sitting there. There was more to it than that. This scene was suddenly so striking because of the sense of 'completion' she added to it. Margo belonged exactly where she was within this living shadow box. She may not have been part of the initial picture but she made her way into it and wore it effortlessly. She knew what she needed and then achieved it without disruption. She, too, found a way.

"Effort is effortless if you are focused."

Startled, I looked around to see who was there, but there was no one within earshot. I glanced Margo's way but she was oblivious to my presence as she lovingly scanned the tops of her new evergreen neighbors with immense delight. It wasn't her. And it wasn't me. So…

"If you cannot see then it is up to you to readjust the telescope within your hand. Unless, of course, it is blindness that you seek."

Dailies

Then I knew. I quietly laughed to myself. "Because I'm the one who put it out of focus in the first place, right Robert?" He didn't answer. He didn't have to. I knew it was him. He's my own American Express card because I can't seem to leave home without him. "So, I've been trying too hard? Is that it?" Nothing. "Am I not trying hard enough?" More nothing. My only response was the sound of the wind blowing through the limbs and leaves above me. I wasn't really surprised at his silence. That's how it works. I would have been more shocked if he'd actually said something else. "Fine. Don't tell me anything. See if I care." I knew my flip commentary didn't help the situation but I am a creature of extreme habit.

"Watch her."

"Oh, fine, Robert. Prove me wrong," I thought to myself and to any collective energy that happened to be scanning my frequency at that particular moment. "Watch her do what?" I was again embraced by knowledgeable silence. With a shrug of well-known defeat, I turned my attention back to Margo of the Forest. She was still taking in her surroundings like a lord surveying his land. I raised my camera as she looked my way. That unfaltering smile was still in place and I managed to capture it. I laughed, "You belong there." Then it hit me like a ton of Twinkies.

All of a sudden, with three little words, I had answered my own ageless question: Where do I belong? I have meandered through a life where, more times than not, I did not feel comfortable in my own skin. From early elementary school through the half-century mark I've always felt that I was the odd man out. One could say I just wasn't on the same page as those around me when, in reality, I was spending most of my time in a completely different library. On those far and few between occasions when I felt at ease someone else would manage to make a point to remind me of my own awkward displacement. Seeing Margo in what could best be described as 'in her natural surroundings,' I knew that I really do belong right here. I don't mean within the Muir Woods (how can one live anywhere without direct access to cheesecake?). I mean right here, within myself. The very place I had pretty much abandoned due to lack of comfort and joy. Instead of constantly rearranging the furniture all I had to do was be grateful for what I have and utilize it all to my maximum comfort. Or, as Robert and the Gang like to say, for my "best and highest."

Out of habit I would run and hide, cutting myself off from anyone within ear's reach, whenever my discomfort and depression became too intense. Margo was comfortable where she was sitting because she was happy being. She was who she was no matter where she happened to be at the time. I realized that what I needed to do was simply readjust. I had to find a way—to *be* the way—and the way *is* acceptance.

I glanced back up to see Margo reluctantly starting her decent back to earth. She steadied herself on one tree with her right hand as her left jutted out to the side for balance. My first thought was that she was the world's first All Natural Tightrope Walker. The focused look on her face was evidence of her mind marking out an evacuation route back down the hillside. I could nearly see a Family Circus-like dotted line marking her projected trail. I walked over to the base of the embankment directly beneath her and extended my hand.

"Do you need some help?" This time my inquiry didn't fall on stubbornly deaf ears. She took my hand, and, working together, she finished her trek back to the trail. She laughed lightly, but I could sense a vague disappointment that she didn't do it all on her own. Like me, she's not one for asking for assistance. It's not pride as much as it is having embraced self-reliance at an early age.

"Nice to get help from time to time, huh?" I snorted.

"You merely have to ask for it." (My, but Robert's become a chatty fellow all of a sudden.)

"It's not always that easy," Margo replied as she mindlessly slapped dirt from her jeans.

"Don't I know it," I answered back. "Most times I just can't."

She turned and looked up at me, those turquoise eyes of hers deliberately drilling right into my very soul. She said so-matter-of-factly, "I hate *'I can'ts'*. There's always a way to achieve what you're after, what you want. It just depends on how badly you want it, how hard you're willing to work for it and what you're willing to sacrifice." She readjusted the bag on her shoulder without her eyes leaving mine. "You've gotta take yourself seriously if you want anyone else to."

Well dip me in butter and fry my butt.

* * *

How do you like that? After months of sitting in the dark, a lone, impassioned statement, a mere conglomeration of letters, pulled the window shade up with one violent jerk. The rays came crashing through with a blinding reality. I can't really exclaim the overused adage, *'I have seen the light!'* But I can say my own shadow was blocking a lot from my own view. My anger, my discomfort, my stubborn refusal to just wholly accept myself had been blocking oh-so-many roadways. At just the prospect, the mere hint, of removing *'I can't'* from my vernacular I was already seeing road barricades being tossed aside with wild abandon.

Before you ask, no, it was not 'that easy.' All change, no matter how good it may be, is hard. The reality of the change, however, was embarrassingly simple.

It really is amazing to me how we can become adjusted to living in the dark so effortlessly. Accepting the drudgery without much of a fight while putting so much of our precious energy into looking away is, frankly, just plain stupid. Believe me, I know. I'm the official mascot of this mindset. My Guides must spend a lot of their time shaking their heads in dismay at my sightless stubbornness. I can only assume The Other Side includes a great healthcare package that covers group whiplash.

I stood there on the dirt path in dumbfounded silence trying to figure it all out again. My soul had already put two and two together and was now impatiently waiting for my tiny mortal brain to catch up. I craned my neck to see with clarity, perhaps for the first time, exactly where I was standing. I was surrounded by these living, deeply-rooted mammoths that were there long before my entrance into this life and, I'm sure, will continue long after I've passed. I was positively dwarfed by their presence, both physically and energetically. And I had dared to think I was the center of my own Universe? What on earth was I thinking? I shook my head, quietly chuckling to myself. Thinking isn't what needs to be done, especially in a place like that. Feeling is what is desired. The heart fuels the truth in knowledge. The mind, while perfectly capable of long division, is actually clueless when it comes to truly important matters. And I had permitted myself to forget. "Way to go," I thought. I was just stunned. Margo had made it all seem so straightforward. And, to her credit, that's exactly what it was.

Once again, like clockwork, Margo's voice brought me back. "Are you coming or not?" She was looking back over her shoulder, already several steps down the trail. Even at fifty paces the heart in her eyes was loud and clear.

"You bet I am," I said. And I started walking forward again.

* * *

Later that evening I sat at my desk, flicked on the lamp and pulled out a pad of legal paper. I pulled out a pencil—a Staedtler 3B in case you were wondering—and reintroduced it to my hand. The light from the lamp playfully bounced over the graphite path forming across the paper. Instead of toying with what was coming out I just enjoyed the familiarity of the flow of it all. The flow of the line, the flow of the words, the flow of life. The paper and pencil, as well as my fingertips, were encased in the illumination of creation and life while the back of my hand, and the paper beyond it, remained in the shadows of what was yet to be. And I'll find that out soon enough.

Where do you go for direction? Don't bother answering because it's an absurd question. It's different for everyone. The importance is, from my own experiences, knowing that direction is being given. And, on some level, you are taking notes as you put one foot in front of the other. When someone tells you a joke do you sit and try to understand why the joke is being told or do you just laugh out of instinct? When you hear a sad story do you have to digest all aspects of it before opting for a response or do you automatically cry? You don't think, you feel. You *are* without knowing *why* and yet you accept it, yourself, as part of the package of life.

Dailies

I have been very blessed with my awareness of my Spirit Guides in my life. They crashed through my wall like the Kool-Aid Guy from the beginning. Don't worry if you don't believe your Guides work with you in the same bombastic way. Trust me when I tell you they are there at your side working with you in the manner that is for your best and highest. Remember, Robert & Company didn't make their presence known to me until I was three-quarters of the way through my 40th year. Either that was the Master Plan or it took them that long to work up the nerve to talk to me.

Lay your map out before you and flip on your lamp, folks. Let's get this show on the road.

Dailies _____

20___

Day-To-Day Reminders _____

"Who's Who: The Guides Guide"

"I'm astounded by people who want to 'know' the universe when it's hard enough to find your way around Chinatown."
— **Woody Allen**

TO HELP GIVE YOU A BETTER INSIGHT into my Spirit Peeps, here's your very own Team Roster:

Robert is my Master Guide, the foreman of the construction crew. He pretty much oversees the others (and one can only assume he handles all of their on-going complaints about my obtuse ways). He is the first one that I officially met. He introduced himself to me through an exercise in automatic writing in December 2002. He is the main voice of my crew. He always opens and closes each channeling and/or automatic writing session. He's wise and funny, and he has a way of bringing a tear to my eye followed by a burst of laughter. Even though he is the one that I interact with most, he is the one about which I know the least. He's very close-mouthed about himself. He will usually respond to my barrage of inquiries with a joke. For example, when I asked when he last physically walked the earth, he said, "Let's just say I had a pet dinosaur." When I kept pushing the matter, he said, "This is not vital to your growth." Then he shut up until I moved beyond it. He knows exactly how to get my attention even while I'm sleeping. He will often come to me within my dreams as Robert Stack from TV's *Unsolved Mysteries*.

My other guides have given me brief glimpses into their physical appearance, but Robert, in his never-ending quest to be different, has not. He is purposely close-lipped and, I have to wholeheartedly admit, it drives me crazy. However, I've had two distinguished psychics give me the same physical descriptions of Robert on two separate and totally unrelated occasions. I've been told Robert is slender in stature and stands around 6'3". He has a prominent hawk-like nose and a thick, dark handlebar mustache. His eyes, in contrast, are a very light slate gray in color. His dark hair is long and swept back over his head and down his neck, covering his starched white collar. He also wears a long dark duster coat with equally dark slacks and shoes. It makes sense, doesn't it? That I, with my obsessive love of cemeteries, would end up with a spirit guide that resembles a monochromatic old west mortician.

Laura is my Protector Guide. She is petite—around 5'5"—with shoulder length jet black hair. There is a simple gold band around her head. This band holds an oval red jewel of some kind in place just above her third eye. She made her presence known to me as I watched the classic film noir masterpiece, *Laura*, starring Gene Tierney. So, in my mind, she looks a lot like Ms. Tierney. Translation: she's a hottie! I am told she was a Third-Level Priestess in Atlantis. Her loving energy is intoxicating. I can feel her around me, especially during stressful situations, and she always manages to soothe my nerves. I've even felt her hug me. Yes, I *felt* her hug me. It is this solid, loving embrace that nearly defies description. She is kind, loving, and gentle…except when I am in some sort of danger. At that point she changes from this angelic soul to a tigress protecting her cubs! Do not mess with this chick.

Case in point: in January 2006, I had a heart attack. I was in my hospital room waiting to be taken into surgery. The doctors were telling me they did not really know the extension of the damage yet, but they were hoping all it would take to fix me up would be the insertion of a stent. A bypass was, however, still a possibility. So, needless to say, I was a neurotic mess.

I sat there, in a chair clearly snagged at a random roadside motel Going-Out-Of-Business sale, sending out one last-ditch plea to my Spirit Guides. I have never been one for any ritualistic behavior, so my "prayers" are merely stated commentary. I told them that while the spiritual side of me may be more understanding of what's going on, the physical side of me truly needed some encouragement. "I really need a sign from you that everything's going to be okay!" I said within. "Especially you, Laura! I really need you here!"

Suddenly a woman out in the hospital corridor yelled loudly and clearly, "Hi, Laura!"

And everything was A-okay.

Martin, my Life Guide, is a Russian Cossack. He's huge. 6'5" or taller. He has thick, dark red hair with a matching beard. His barrel chest is covered in what looks like fur—a vest perhaps. He is very jovial and fun loving. He speaks in broken English that makes me think I'm channeling Boris Badenov. Martin likes to flirt with women and has a craving for, of all things, White Russians. He tells me we were brothers in a physical incarnation. When I asked him, "If we were brothers why are you there and I am still here?" He laughed and said, "Because our mother always liked me best!" There's your first lesson, kids. Sibling rivalry is inescapable.

Christopher, whose primary role is guiding me with my writing, is a Tibetan Monk with ADHD. Seriously. When he's around I am overly hyper and can be easily distracted by my surroundings in a way that makes me want to take everything

Dailies

in at once. But when it's time to actually write—to focus—our combined energy completely changes. We meld into one totally driven force and all of those earlier "distractions" are nowhere to be found. He's short, bald and has Marty Feldman's bulging eyes. Honestly, he reminds me of Uncle Fester from The Addam's Family. No shock there.

Pamela is an olive skinned, full-lipped gypsy beauty. She's also a chain smoker. Oh, sure, she says she's a reformed smoker but I don't believe it for a second. Whenever I channel her I find myself holding my hand as if I'm cradling a cigarette. She is brutally direct and she refuses to put up with my crap. She calls me on it all the time and, honestly, I'm grateful that she does. I can't get away with anything with her. Excuses are unacceptable, end of story. When she first appeared on the scene, she told me that she would be helping with my understanding of the tarot. If that's the case she needs to file for unemployment because the tarot makes no more sense to me than women. Of course, while the tarot continues to baffle me, I do have a seemingly natural connection with most Oracle Cards. Go figure.

It was after her appearance that I discovered that the artist behind the classic Waite-Smith tarot deck was none other than Pamela Colman Smith. When this bit of information came across my desk the hair on the back of my neck stood on end. Was that Pamela my Spirit Guide? In meditation I asked her this. She replied, "No, but I had you going for a minute, didn't I?" What's not to love? If she were here in the physical I would probably propose marriage based solely on her flip comment. That says a lot about my selection process, doesn't it?

Oliver reminds me of Sebastian Cabot from the TV series, *Family Affair*. He gives me the impression of someone who would be a Head Master at an upper class private school in

New England. Obviously, his role in this cast of characters is to assist me in my own teaching endeavors. I pity him for that. I truly loathe teaching. On those rare occasions when I do it I am miserable virtually the entire time. I admittedly understand the origin of my disdain toward teaching. Growing up, I hated school with every fiber of my being. I resented being told what to do and how to do it, and I hated "serving my time" with all of those so-called peers of mine of which no close relations were ever made. It wasn't a happy time for me, and my taking on the role of teacher just pulls all of those memories back to the surface. Of course, I could look at it as a way to change the process that I begrudgingly went through and turn it into a positive scenario for all involved… NAAAAAA!

I can only assume Oliver has come down with some sort of nervous disorder by now.

The One Who Soars with Eagles is a relatively young Native American guide. I have a feeling he would be no more than 25 years of physical age. I don't think he was a Chief, but he still had some prominent placement within the tribal leadership. I believe he is a member of the Hopi tribe. I don't have any proof of this tiny bit of trivia about him, it's just a gut feeling that I have. And if I have learned anything from my interactions with my crew it's to just go with that intuitive nudge from beyond.

I was pulled to Sedona, Arizona for our introductory meeting. The initial "conversation" took place, as with most of my Guides, via an automatic writing session. Oliver lured me to The Chapel of the Holy Cross, a non-denominational church designed by Frank Lloyd Wright, with a simplistic yet cryptic phrase, "Eagles. Go with the eagles." When I asked what he meant by the statement he merely replied oh-so-very smugly, "You'll find out." And I did. As I sat outside of the chapel, I

Dailies

turned to face a rock formation that was unmistakably the head of an eagle. Once inside, with pad and pen in hand, he began to speak to me. One of the things he told me that day sticks with me through thick and thin: "In order to teach you must free your mind of unnecessary baggage and weight, for that will only limit you. Prejudice and ignorance have no place in the classroom. Do not forget 'life' is a classroom." Admittedly, that is not the easiest thing to do when fatigued and frustrated, but I do my best. Or at least, I try to believe that I do.

Dondi is a small boy—approximately 7 or 8 years of age—and is the spitting image of his comic strip namesake. His role is simple: helping me keep the youthful joy of my so-called inner-child alive and well in all that I do. I would like to point out that I'm being reminded that this is the approach I should take with my teaching, but I am opting to ignore it. Aren't I clever? How perfect is it that a cartoonist, who is an adoptee, gets a comic strip orphan as a guide? I guess Annie was already booked.

Thomas is here to keep me on my spiritual pathway. He wears sunglasses, khakis and Hawaiian print shirts. He speaks fluent sarcasm and has the knack of hitting a nail on the head at forty paces. He is also the only guide who first came to me in a dream.

In this dream I was standing in an open, white space filled with brilliant light and just enough mist to make me wonder if someone had left the dry ice machine turned on. I was standing across from a middle-aged guy who reminded me of a clichéd beach community resident. I couldn't really tell if he was barefoot or if he wore flip-flops, but I was sure his feet hadn't played host to a legitimate pair of shoes in quite some time. He was jovial, extroverted and loud. I liked him instantly. He was explaining to me that he was one of my Spirit Guides and he was determined to keep me headed due north along my spiritual journey. I finally asked him my predictable question, "But what is your name?"

He laughed, of course, and handed me a Thomas Guide, the honest-to-God Bible of Roads along the west coast. I literally woke up laughing.

And finally, there's **Joseph**, a most mysterious wanderer. While Thomas is here to keep me *on* my path, it is Joseph who works ahead of the game in order to keep the way as clear of useless debris as possible. When new guides are about to make themselves known to me, I always begin feeling something unusual about the energy surrounding me. Something a bit indescribable will start feeling out of sorts. It's almost like being in an elevator when one too many people gets in the car. You find yourself adjusting your position in order to make room for the new passenger and, at first, it's a bit awkward. After a couple of days of this lightweight intrusion everything evens out again and I find myself with another mouth at the table.

As I began getting accustomed to the latest change of energy around me I heard the name, "Joseph." And, as always, I questioned the information. My people know this—and I like to think they consider this a delightful eccentricity on my part—and they always come through to validate it for me. This time, however, they went beyond the call of duty. I was sitting in my car after finishing a day of private readings in Anaheim, California. I was relaxing, grounding myself and doing my best to release all the information that had passed through me over the past few hours. My tranquility was broken when someone rapped on the passenger window. I slowly opened my eyes as I turned my head toward the unwelcome sound. Never one to hide my feelings I'm sure my face was encased with an

Dailies

expression of pure displeasure. I saw a small, stocky Latino man standing there. He was clad in a once discarded olive green coat that was far from secondhand. He looked disheveled, his dark hair peeking out intermittently from under a well-worn cap. His face clearly hadn't seen a razor in some time. Despite his downtrodden appearance there was a kindness in his eyes that canceled all other judgments that briefly entered my mind. Without hesitation I pushed the button on my door, lowering the passenger window.

"Excuse me," he said softly. "I'm sorry for bothering you but I'm trying to feed my family." He pointed over his shoulder without breaking eye-contact with me. "Can you spare any change?"

I looked in the direction he pointed and saw a petite woman in equally dark, tattered clothes holding a toddler in her arms. The child was blissfully sleeping with his head resting on his mother's shoulder.

I could not shake his eyes. I merely nodded and handed him five dollars. He took it as one corner of his mouth curled upward in a gentle smile. He placed the bill in his coat pocket then extended his hand in order to shake mine. "God bless you, sir," he said simply.

"And you," I replied.

"What is your name? I would like to add you to our family's prayers."

I'm ashamed that I was a little shocked at his request. "Charles," I said. "And yours?"

"Joseph," he said still smiling. I hope my jaw smashing onto the car seat didn't break the mood for him.

I watched him walk back to his wife and child. He put his arm lovingly, protectively, around his family and they walked down the street. I just sat there in stunned silence for a bit longer than originally intended. I'm telling you, folks, there are miracles taking place around us daily. Sometimes you have to hunt for them. Other times they come rap-rap-rapping on your window. So make a point to answer.

Dailies _____

30

Day-To-Day Reminders _____

January 1

"Life is about change, new beginnings, lessons learned and shared. While cycles may end rest assured that the love within the lessons never does."

— Robert

Dailies _____

JANUARY 2

"Peace is possible. Peace is attainable. Peace is as real as you permit it to be. Only YOU know YOUR peace. No one should interfere with your tranquility nor should you try to topple theirs."

— Robert

January 3

"We are all equal yet walking completely different pathways. Wouldn't it make more sense to watch your own step instead of attempting to govern your neighbor's stride?"

– Robert

Dailies _____

January 4

"The heart sees with compassion and depth. The mind makes up the facts as it goes along. It is up to you to keep your sight in check."

— Martin

Day-To-Day Reminders _____

JANUARY 5

"An unmade bed is just as comfortable as one neatly tucked in — do not permit the judgments and opinions of others, majority notwithstanding, dictate YOUR comfort."

– Robert

JANUARY 6

"In the annals of time there are many corridors, many doors, many rooms. The depth of knowledge there is overwhelming, to say the least. But the one lone common denominator is that of basic truth. The mind of man tends to clutter that aspect up with such things as judgmental attempts at undeserved control and unnecessarily ritualistic hoop-jumping. Accept, in your heart, what is YOUR truth and live by that creed."

— Robert

January 7

"Until you fully grasp the power of your ability you will never fully understand the infinite possibilities within your reach."

— Robert

Dailies _____

January 8

"Your own limitations are only set by the confines of your mind."

— Robert

Day-To-Day Reminders _____

January 9

"Grasp the brass ring. It is right there within your reach. It will shine, it will glisten, and it will never lose its brilliance providing you never loosen your grip."

– Robert

Dailies _____

January 10

"Never forget the heart of who you are. Return to the love and the light and reassure those around you that the light is always on and that it always warms the essence of their soul."

– Robert

Day-To-Day Reminders _____

JANUARY 11

"All you do and say and think is part of your lesson. Let go of the anger. It doesn't get you anywhere. Do this and you will find the path easier, less confusing. Get rid of the excess and keep only the staples. All journeys need the proper preparation. Anything extra weighs you down. It is not what you need, it is not critical."

– Oliver

Dailies _____

January 12

"Make sure your foundation is solid before adding more floors."

— Robert

Day-To-Day Reminders _____

JANUARY 13

"What others think of you is not important. What you do for others is."

— Robert

Dailies _____

January 14

"The power of the divine white light is, in fact, centered within you. Keep it on at all times for all to see more clearly for it is only in the darkness of lies that one will falter and trip."

— Robert

January 15

"There is a process and, trust me when I tell you, we know what we are talking about. We have been dead much longer than you have been alive. You can say we have this down to a science. So, you say, 'I must trust you then?' And I say, 'You must first trust yourself . Once you do that everything else will slip into place.' Trust, my friend. Trust and so much will be open to you, your heart included."

— Martin

Dailies _____

JANUARY 16

"Arrange your life so that it best suits your path. Do not try to fit the path through your life. Don't make the pieces fit. Simply find the pieces that fit. You will know."

— Robert

Day-To-Day Reminders _____

January 17

"A book has a beginning, middle and end for a reason. There are stages to the plot just as there are stages to your life. You cannot put one chapter in front of another and still have it make sense. Read your book in the order that it is written, for then the climax will be all the more significant. Not only to you but to those who are learning from it."

— Robert

Dailies _____

JANUARY 18

"Do not allow successes or failures to cloud your judgment. Each moment is new and each moment holds infinite possibilities. Merely tie one moment to the next in order to create a straight, solid path."

— Robert

January 19

"The sum of all parts is the soul within as well as the souls that you touch."

– Robert

Dailies _____

JANUARY 20

"The absurdity of asking the classic stupid question is the saddest comedy of man."

— *The One Who Soars with Eagles*

Day-To-Day Reminders _____

JANUARY 21

"Spiritual spring cleaning is necessary. It is refreshing. It is as if you are being reborn. The promise of a new day. A new adventure. A new dawn. A new light. The wonder within these prospects will never cease to amaze you. You must walk farther and discover not only all that you can but all that you have."

– Robert

Dailies _____

January 22

"You cannot force what is not meant to be."

– Robert

Day-To-Day Reminders _____

January 23

"Do not deliver anger at the feet of those who believe differently. You do not believe as everyone does. There is no wrong way to love; therefore there is no right way. To indicate a "right way" one is saying there is but one way. There are many ways as there are thoughts. Each form of love is as pure and true as the next."

– The One Who Soars with Eagles

January 24

"It is always the trailblazers who question their own path. It is hard to see what is ahead while walking in unchartered territory. And yet you continue to move forward. Do not feel bad when you slip and fall. It is always the falls that teach you why you are standing in the first place."

– Robert

JANUARY 25

"It matters not where you reside for you only truly live within yourself."

— Robert

January 26

"Listen with your soul and you will hear all there is."

— Robert

January 27

"Love and compassion always burn though the darkness but it becomes even brighter when it is joined by true understanding. As the night falls around you know you shall never be encased in darkness. Your light will enlighten many but do not forget to let your own light lead the way for yourself as well."

—Robert

January 28

"Look out over the sea and what do you see on the horizon? Don't you DARE say 'nothing.' If you saw truly saw nothing then you would see just that: NOTHING. You see water. You see sky. You see clouds. Birds, perhaps? Where are they flying? Who knows at this point? Do you think all destinations are set ahead of time? No. The horizon is seemingly infinite for a reason: BECAUSE IT IS. Your potential is infinite."

— Robert

January 29

"Everything has a value. Sometimes we have to struggle to find it."

— Robert

Dailies _____

January 30

"Be the person that you are, not the person you THINK you are. Your reality is within your hands. Allow it to breathe and thrive. Like a butterfly let it soar swiftly, elegantly and with beauty. Open your palm and release the butterfly from its cocoon."

– Robert

Day-To-Day Reminders _____

January 31

"Even when your pocket is seemingly empty you should be quietly grateful that you have a pocket in the first place."

— Thomas

FEBRUARY 1

"Life is not empty. If you're filling your tank with sadness I really suggest you try another pump. Far be it from me to tell you what to do but—and I'm just thinkin' out loud here—if I were getting lousy mileage on my path I'd sure as Shinola be upgrading to supreme. We have choices for a reason. You can choose to improve or you can run along on nothing but fumes. Your choice: Your call."

— *Thomas*

FEBRUARY 2

"When you hear the phrase 'time is of the essence' you may as well laugh to yourself for it is 'love' and 'life' that is essential. Time is merely a way to measure it. Do not be concerned with the measurement. Merely be concerned with the fact that you have it and that you cherish it and that you live it."

— Robert

Dailies _____

FEBRUARY 3

"There is nothing wrong with Christianity. The problem lies within the malpractioners of it."

— The One Who Soars with Eagles

FEBRUARY 4

"In wisdom there lies question. Were it not for the initial question, from where would you derive your wisdom? Doubt is healthy. An abundance of doubt is laziness."

– *The One Who Soars with Eagles*

FEBRUARY 5

"Food is essential for survival. I speak of food for the body, for the mind, for the spirit, for the soul. How do you expect to live without it? You can exist without a proper diet but, I ask you, why would you want to merely exist when you can LIVE!"

— Robert

FEBRUARY 6

"I ask that you look within yourself for the strength and focus on what you are seeking. It is said that the best way to hide something is within plain view. I assure you this is the case with you. It is right there before your eyes, within your heart."

— Robert

Dailies _____

FEBRUARY 7

"There is no night. There is no day. There is merely what there is. Obsessing on measuring "what is" with the ticking of the clock or crossing off blocks of a calendar removes the focus—the appreciation—of "what is." Appreciate the now for you will remember it then in order to get to the next plateau."

— Christopher

FEBRUARY 8

"Focus on the love and on the energy for it cannot guide you wrong. Feel the energy and let it become your beacon. I will not let you lose your grounding; your footing. Walk with me, stand tall with me, and we will face the winds with confidence and love."

— Laura <u>69</u>

FEBRUARY 9

"In order to teach you must free your mind of unnecessary baggage and weight for that will only limit you. Prejudice and ignorance have no place in the classroom. Do not forget 'life' is a classroom."

– The One Who Soars with Eagles

FEBRUARY 10

"Everlasting light will shine from within your heart. You may scoff at the goodness within you but it is there and you know it. Look within yourself – your true self – and you will be blinded by the radiance in you…"

– Robert

February 11

"Do you pick up your phone in order to connect, communicate or share with another? Or is it just the opposite? Is it a way to reach another or merely a distraction from what surrounds you? Productive or destructive? Progression or regression? Sharing or segregation? It is literally your call."

– Thomas

February 12

"Have faith for faith will carry you above the clouds of doubt and despair providing a view that is more breathtaking than that of the highest eagle."

— Robert

February 13

"Faith has nothing to do with merely believing for the sake of believing. Faith DOES NOT falter BUT your theory and rationalization of it does. As a river swirls and swerves, altering the terrain it passes over and by; your faith does the same to your own soul, your own acceptance. Allow the river to carry you back to your faith and embrace the changes within."

– Robert

February 14

"If you can give of your own heart freely—if you can share the simplicity of the purity of your own being—then what greater gift can there possibly be? Take the hand of those around you, as you would a small child, and show them the wonderment of the love not only within you but within themselves. Do not do this because of *the season*. Make this gift your *reason*."

— Robert

Dailies _____

FEBRUARY 15

"Your garden will only be as beautiful as you allow it. But it is best to have your garden reach its full potential. One flower may be lovely but a garden full of flowers is far more eye catching and will be seen by so many more people. Share the beauty."

– Robert

February 16

"In a classroom you have many tools of education at your fingertips. Books, worksheets, tests, pop quizzes, and of course, teachers. It is up to you how you utilize these tools. You can read a book or you can burn it. It's in your hands. The hand is a way to reach out to others. Pass what you know on to the next and so on: a chain that will go on for many generations and connect one era to the next as one."

— Oliver

February 17

"You will get a better look at all you have done by standing back and seeing just how much distance you have covered. A proper perspective is best achieved when the plane of view is seen in its entirety for then you can see where you began, where you are and where you will be."

— Robert

February 18

"The goodness lies within and it journeys out at your control, much like a shadow. The higher the light the greater distance the shadow will cover. Let your goodness reach like the longest shadow of the tallest tree."

– Robert

FEBRUARY 19

"An artist must prepare his canvas prior to creating the wondrous beauty from his hand. Treat your canvas as you are about to embark on your own Sistine Chapel."

– Robert

FEBRUARY 20

"It is best to give a gift anonymously than to have your name etched into a brass plaque on a wall. Eventually, the brass will tarnish. The wall will crumble. The impact you have on the human soul never fades. It will stand the test of time against all elements for truth defies all negativity and comes forth in the dawn of the new day."

– Robert

Dailies _____

FEBRUARY 21

"You must find the answers through your meditations. There, within the infinite walls of hope and faith, you will find the solace of knowledge and truth."

— Robert

Day-To-Day Reminders _____

February 22

"Enlighten me so I may better see and hear."

— Laura

Dailies _____

FEBRUARY 23

"You have the pieces of the puzzle. Put them together. Form the picture-perfect reality before you, piece by piece, and let THAT be your truth. It IS your future providing YOU believe it is before you."

— Robert

Day-To-Day Reminders _____

February 24

"The only reason to look back is to see how far you've come."

— Robert

FEBRUARY 25

"Remain steadfast in your faith and this will keep your feet secured to the ground even in the harshest wind. Be aware of the power within a prayer. It can withstand the strongest of opposition and it is the lightest weapon to carry."

– Robert

February 26

It is not important what you THINK you have learned or not learned. Each experience is a lesson. It is up to you what you derive from it.

— Robert

February 27

"Observations are elaborate distractions. Notice, do not dwell. Acknowledge, do not wander. Realize, do not lose focus. Excuses are easily made. Facts cannot be hidden but they can be ignored. What do you intend to do?"

– Robert

February 28

"A breeze, whether at your back or in your face, will encircle you. It will either blow dust in your face or cool you on a hot day. It is your free will to choose whether to protect your eyes and face the direction it leads you or go into it head on illogically unprotected. God protects… ignorance does not."

— Robert

FEBRUARY 29

"We remember vividly the years of blindness. We are joyous now celebrating within the light around you as well as emitting from you. Join us in the celebration. Do not let yourself get caught up in what you consider to be failures. You are just learning. All toddlers fall before running. You are no different. Get back up and run again."

– Robert

MARCH 1

"A man cannot grow within the confines of a box. The box must be opened into the world outside and, at the same time, never forgetting why he was in the box in the first place. The box will withstand additions. It will not withstand pressures."

—Robert

91

MARCH 2

"Your tapestry of experiences is what creates the outer rhythm of your physical existence. Your bodily mind cannot always see from the eagle's perch. You will not see the reasoning of the pattern of the Divine Seamstress as each stitch is sewn. The effects of the moment do not declare the impact of the outcome. Embrace each lesson you experience as you warm yourself within your life's quilt."

— Robert

MARCH 3

"Remember the power lies within you and you are the power."

— Robert

MARCH 4

"Let the light run free. Allow it to surround, encase, permeate and emit in every possible way. Accept no limitations and your path will always be revealed. But you must remember—and accept—that sometimes clearing the path is part of "the way." Rejoice wherever you are and knowing it IS the right place… it is "home" for the moment."

— Oliver

MARCH 5

"Remember the power of laughter—it is there—it is so strong, it is so strong. And it will lift you up, you see? It will lift you up above the mundane earthly problems and thoughts. For when you are doing the spiritual work those are not important. You are above it. And that is where the laughter elevates you! And it takes you up into the next stratosphere and you feel the energy around you, around others, and you are above the smog, so-to-speak, so you may better see what you need to see."

— Martin

MARCH 6

"A clock measures time. And time is all it takes to measure what you are capable of accomplishing. What time do you have?"

— Robert

March 7

"Open your heart to the vast impossibilities for they ARE possible. Ease your pain with the love that surrounds. That is one of its many functions; many purposes. Think of Love as the DW-40 of the Universe!"

— Thomas

Dailies _____

MARCH 8

"ANOTHER MOMENT IS BUT MERELY ANOTHER CHANCE TO…

You are the one with the pen. You are the One to continue the sentence. May it never end just as none of us never end."

– The One Who Soars with Eagles

Day-To-Day Reminders _____

MARCH 9

"You must stop thinking and begin feeling. Get in touch with yourself—your God Self—and allow that to lead you. It is a fool who will walk into a darkened room and not turn on the light. A wise man will feel for the light switch and turn it on. The light is presented to you; you must find the switch. Turn it on and its radiance will guide you throughout your life."

– Robert

Dailies _____

MARCH 10

"A fork in the road always presents an opportunity. This opportunity can sometimes be clearly marked with a signpost. Other times the signpost is vague. It is up to you to seek within in order to improve your own vision and direction."

– Robert

MARCH 11

"Pristine Awareness allows you to see all surrounding as well as throughout your being. To attain as well as maintain this state you must, with regular regimented determination, keep your lens completely clear. Shine it, polish it, ensure it is as transparent as the truest of hearts. Then there will be no mistaking what is seen…by you as well as of you."

— The Collective

MARCH 12

"Negativity is a lot like early morning fog: the sun eventually breaks through and dissipates the mist. The obstruction of the fog is never permanent because the truth within the light will always break through and warm the soul of the earth."

— Robert

MARCH 13

"I will leave you with this: no matter how insignificant a piece of a puzzle may seem—whether it is a block of blue sky or a dark brown patch of earth—you can't have a complete picture without every single piece."

– Robert

Dailies _____

March 14

"Remember a flower as beautiful as it may appear on the seed packet will not grow to be as beautiful as it could if the garden is not tended to properly. This is your job. Tend to the garden, your garden, so you may grow and bloom and reach toward the sun."

— Robert

March 15

"Be careful of what you say. Remember words last beyond a lifetime. Be aware of the echo coming back from the canyon beyond for it will resonate within the ears of all generations."

— Robert

MARCH 16

"Reality is necessary for it dictates the spirituality within."

– Robert

MARCH 17

"When you embark on a trip there is much preparation. You get maps; you take specific things with you to make the journey easier. Whether clothing, a compass, or any other item you deem as important. Your spiritual journey is no different. Before embarking you must prepare and that is what you are doing now. Plan ahead... and there will be no reason to return home before finishing your journey."

— Robert

Dailies _____

MARCH 18

"All aspirations are manmade. But the achievement is through the Divine Bond. Trust the Hand to be there just as you know yours is there reaching."

— Pamela

MARCH 19

"What is the point of serving others if you have made no place for yourself at the table of gratitude as well?"

— Robert

Dailies _____

MARCH 20

"Words! Allow the words to come from deep within! Listen to your own unique voice! We speak the words but it up to you to believe them! To reiterate them! To share them! If the verbiage does not find the way to the parchment, to the volumes, it is only wasted breath. It is not even an effort! Release the text from the ... inkwell ... set them free ... for your sake as well as the welfare of generations to come!"

— Christopher

MARCH 21

"The truth is perhaps the hardest thing for man to comprehend. It is ambiguous. It is … intangible … yet holds great strength and power. The truth has a way of always surfacing. Spread the truth evenly like a fresh coat of paint. Prime it properly and one coat should suffice. For it is durable, resistant and most beautiful."

<u>111</u>

– Robert

Dailies _____

MARCH 22

"If it feels right within then it will be."

— Robert

MARCH 23

"In your hand is grasped a pen. A pen is merely an instrument; a tool to implant thoughts to paper. You are an instrument, a tool, of God. You are used to put ideas on paper, or energy into reality. The pen is not insignificant. You need it to complete the task; this stage of the Divine Plan. You are the pen to God. Let Him jot through you!"

— Christopher

Dailies _____

MARCH 24

"Remember once something has been carved in stone it is there permanently. Be sure that you provide a permanent vision of truth for all to see."

– Robert

MARCH 25

"A flower starts in the soil and rises to the light. It is proven that when light deprived the flower will seek it out. And, when it does, it blooms. You have many blooms waiting to awaken. Soon it will be a glorious flower bed in which you stand. Looking over it all you will be amazed and you WILL stand tall."

– Robert

MARCH 26

"Do not dwell on what has passed. Look to the future and concentrate on the present. What can you do today that may help someone, and yourself, tomorrow? It is alright to do things for yourself. It is important that you know the difference between helping yourself and being greedy. Have a piece of cake, don't eat the whole thing. Share it."

— Robert

March 27

"Oxygen is a physical form of prayer: it gives life."

— Robert

Dailies _____

MARCH 28

"A man can only travel a road in a vehicle designed for that specific terrain. A bicycle is certainly not ideal for scaling through the Rockies. You need to prepare yourself for your journey. Your diet, your meditations, your prayers, it all works together as a motor for your own personal vehicle."

– Robert

MARCH 29

"Words are heavy so put them in their place gently. This will enable the mortar to firm and make the foundation even stronger."

— Robert

MARCH 30

"A promise is as solid as an oak. It can be cut down but it cannot be forgotten! Just because you cannot touch it or feel it with your fingers does not mean it isn't strong and firm in its roots. The promise grows within you because it was planted there long ago. It is you who has cultivated this grove into what it is today and what it will be in the days to come. Be proud. Be strong. Just as the promise was made for you it is made by you."

— Robert

MARCH 31

"A virtuous man will use his word as a hunter will use his knife. It is necessary, it is a tool of survival, it is a tool of your ethics, morality and immortality."

— Robert

Dailies _____

APRIL 1

"Is it more important to dash through a door without your keys or is it best to check your pockets beforehand? You need to be prepared for the journey as well as the return…just as much as you need to get through the door in the first place."

– Martin

Day-To-Day Reminders _____

April 2

"Art is truly a form of personal expression. How you express yourself is an art. All is displayed for others to see. They interpret it as they see fit. Some get it. Some do not. And this will always be the case. But merely for your own piece of mind and sense of right, you must create your own personal piece of art and many will truly be enamored by it. Beauty and truth speak to the soul."

– Robert

April 3

"You will never understand everything. And the sooner you accept that the easier this will be for you. Some things happen simply because they are meant to be. Whether you approve of them or not, they are meant to be. It is not your position to grasp the situation as it may. It is simply your responsibility to react to it. And how you react to it determines your character."

— Robert

April 4

"Up the ladder, one rung at a time, for if you attempt to jump up or skip a rung it is very likely that you will slide back down. Stay on the ladder and climb to the roof. The view is spectacular. You will see the next horizon and you will see a colorful sunrise that will leave you speechless and simultaneously fill you with great content. Stay on the ladder. It is secure, it will not tip. The only way you can fall is if you let go."

125

— Robert

APRIL 5

"A man will walk with trepidation over a rickety bridge and walk briskly with confidence across a paved road often without looking both ways. Look both ways and always remember where you are headed. The steps in front of you are as crucial as those behind you. Without the ones behind you would not be where you are. And where you are is right with Spirit."

– Robert

APRIL 6

"Learn the ropes; tie the knots correctly to moor the ship of destiny to your dock. It will always be there to sail through life but the security of 'home' will always be at your beck and call. Moor your ship and rejoice in your travels and your homecoming."

— Robert

Dailies _____

APRIL 7

"You are a three dimensional object. A cube is solid. It is ideal for placing things on, enforcing structure and support. A flat two dimensional object, such as paper, offers no support. You cannot put much on it for it will tear; it does not have the strength, the durability. You have to be strong in all three dimensions: spiritually, physically, and emotionally. Without all three you are not solid."

— Robert

APRIL 8

"It is a rainbow that catches your eye. The beginning and ending of it do not matter as much as the beauty before you. No matter how bad things may seem the beauty is always there waiting to viewed."

– Robert

Dailies _____

APRIL 9

"History is important for it not only measures where you have been, it measures the change within you and within the place you call 'home': your heart."

— Robert

<u>130</u>

APRIL 10

"When you are standing on the new mountain top and overlooking the new terrain revealed by the morning sun, always remember the field behind you. Remember when it seemed dark? Yet within that dark seemingly dead field something grew. Something beautiful took root. The sun rising before you was always there peeking through the clouds of your doubt. The clouds are parting. A new day, a new age, is dawning."

— Robert

Dailies _____

April 11

"It never matters how quickly a job is completed. The only thing that matters is the fact that it is completed correctly and in its own time. Everything is done and happens in its own time. Trust God as He is the Master Timekeeper. Always set your watch to the correct time and you will never be late."

– Robert

APRIL 12

"Light encircles you. Feel it. Let the warmth of its radiation penetrate your mind, your body, your spirit. Let the light that you are radiate to others as well as within yourself. It is much easier to see in the darkness when you have a strong, unfaltering light."

– Robert

Dailies _____

APRIL 13

"Be aware of every breath you take and cherish each one as it draws in new and exciting possibilities."

— Robert

Day-To-Day Reminders _____

April 14

"Talk to God as you would a friend. He always hears you and your call is always welcome."

— Robert

Dailies _____

APRIL 15

"The essence of a scripture is the important message within, not the historical value of the content. It is simply a tool used in faith. Your faith can be placed within a bible, a rock, a tree. It truly does not matter as long as you use that bible, rock or tree as an extension from you to God. Religion is merely a ceremony, nothing more. It is a way for people to accept a rather staggering idea."

— Robert

APRIL 16

"God is not, as you say 'as much of a stickler for details' as people think. God is love. God loves you, God believes in you. God merely asks for the same in return. And, believe it or not, even if you don't, God loves you anyway. Unconditional love: THAT is what God is and what God gives. I want you to always remember that. That "other" rhetoric doesn't ring true, you know? It has no soul!"

– Robert & Thomas

Dailies _____

April 17

"Guidance is always needed by the teacher and the student. It is a mutual process of exchange and learning. One does not exclusively lead and one does not exclusively follow. Give and take. Remember: it IS a wise man who understands the significance as well as the similarity of teaching and being taught."

– Oliver

April 18

"Quiet the mind, calm the spirit…let your soul reach out and speak."

— Laura

Dailies _____

April 19

"Discard the past. Do not forget it."

— Martin

Day-To-Day Reminders _____

April 20

"A deck of cards fans out. You do the same, you know? Your aura, your energy, fans out to others. The people will reach in and pull out what they need from you. But always remember this: what they take is only what YOU freely give."

– Pamela

April 21

"The life path is one of turmoil and joy. You must learn to adapt and cope with it all. It is, at the risk of sounding like broken record, all part of learning. And trust me, that never ends. You are always learning something. But it does become easier. With the learning comes acceptance. And acceptance brings you peace which is what I wish for you, my friend."

— Martin

APRIL 22

"All life is essential, from your brothers to the trees on the far-off horizon. To pollute Mother Earth is to pollute your very soul. Live Green—the Green of growth, the Green of healing. Nurture the Nature where you breathe, where you stand, where you live! What better way to teach the significance of all life to future generations?"

— The One Who Soars with Eagles

Dailies _____

APRIL 23

"Faith is the easiest thing in the world... except, sadly, when it is directed at ourselves."

— Joseph

<u>144</u>

Day-To-Day Reminders _____

APRIL 24

"Remember: simply because you want something does not mean it is what needs to be."

– Robert

Dailies _____

APRIL 25

"You must be comfortable and accepting of your own wants, your own desires, your own needs, your own passions. If you are not comfortable enough to announce them then how can you adjust to them once they are presented to you?"

— Robert

April 26

"Like the water that flows freely and swiftly from stream to river to ocean your understanding will reach many and quench the thirsts of all who drink from it—yourself included."

– Robert

147

April 27

"Look within your heart where a flame burns with everlasting love and passion. That flame is the source of energy for you. When the flame dims due to lack of fuel you weaken and slow down. You must properly fuel the flame. Teachings tell us the burning bush revealed God's plan to Moses. The flame within you reveals God's plan to you."

— Robert

APRIL 28

"Man has placed much negativity with fire. It is misinterpreted by so many. A fire provides warmth, it can cook your food, it can lighten the darkest cavern. However, if misused, it can destroy, and burn all life in its path until there is nothing but a dark cold black abyss. How many times have people killed others all in the name of God? That is blasphemous. Too much of a good thing is indeed a good thing. But when it is misused that is where the danger lies. Feed your fire with love and truth. Provide the right nutrition and your fire will burn as long and enlighten as far as all eyes can see."

– Robert

Dailies _____

APRIL 29

"The key to being all that you can be is simply being comfortable with all that you are."

— *The One Who Soars with Eagles*

150

APRIL 30

"A simple prayer reminds those who have passed that they are still loved by those on this side of the veil. They do not forget their lives and loves in the physical world by any means. A prayer comforts them, brings a warm memory to them and helps them to become stronger spiritually. The stronger they become the more they accomplish which will help them when they return to your plane or move on to the next."

— Robert

Dailies _____

MAY 1

"You can see best through your own lenses—those you clean yourself—and not the eyeglasses of others."

– Robert

__152__

Day-To-Day Reminders _____

MAY 2

"Remember you and Spirit are one. It's like two halves. You take one half and put it together with the other half and you have the whole. You are not whole without Spirit; Spirit is not whole without you. Why? Because Spirit loves you. And what good is love if you cannot share it with someone else? Remember: one half with another half creates wholeness: wholeness within one and one within all."

— Laura

May 3

"To doubt demonstrates that you are thinking, processing, experiencing. When you allow doubt to take over then you have stopped living freely in mind and spirit. Life's journey requires all senses. Heighten them! Exercise them! If you do not like broccoli do you stop eating all together? Or do you merely dine on something else? Doubt feeds you. Giving in to doubt results in spiritual starvation."

– Joseph

MAY 4

"You will never learn from a book what lives within your heart. Believe what you know is truth, not someone else's variation of it."

— Oliver

Dailies _____

MAY 5

"Words may seem like feathers, virtually weightless as they blow along your way. But, when accumulated, the feathers can soar to the heavens... or they can blow apart and plummet. Where do your words and intent go? That, dear child, is up to you."

— The One Who Soars with Eagles

May 6

"Guide as you wish to be guided. Love as you wish to be loved. Be as you wish to be."

— Christopher

Dailies _____

MAY 7

"Inspiration can fuel you but it is your individuality that will carry you."

— Robert

Day-To-Day Reminders _____

MAY 8

"Do not think of us as Spiritual Visitors but merely old friends reuniting once more. Those of us in Spirit are as excited over the prospect of communication with you as you are with us! We are not deities. We are simply Beings of Light, just as yourselves, sharing our Universal Love and all the prospects that come with it."

— Robert

Dailies _____

MAY 9

"Faith is not about understanding. It is about knowing."

— Laura

Day-To-Day Reminders _____

May 10

"All patterns can be broken. It is up to the individual. You cannot create a quilt without a pattern. But not all quilts are the same. Sew the pattern that best suits you and find comfort beneath it."

— Robert

May 11

"The strength of truth; the durability of love; there is nothing better or more overwhelming!"

— Robert

May 12

"You have been given the gift of self trust. Utilize it."

— Robert

Dailies _____

MAY 13

"Trust yourself. It is time to remove the training wheels. It is time to GO forward…GO upward…GO inward. It is time to get on the elevator and rise to the potential within. For it is there, within you, where true greatness resides."

— Robert

May 14

"The sketch pad before you has many pages. The possibilities for the contents are staggering and unlimited by only your own desires. It is up to you to fill these pages. You have the eraser, you have the lead. Use them as you see fit. What feels right to you? What… feels… right… to… YOU?"

– Robert

May 15

"You may find your own enlightenment seemingly too bright; your normal desire will be to shield your eyes from it. Do not. To do this is to deny who you are! To do so is to deny living! It's all part of the same package so utilize it all. Ease into the song and join the chorus that is your Spiritual Guidance and Soul Purpose!"

– Robert

May 16

"There is truly no room for doubt. Unless, of course, you open the door and usher it right in."

— Joseph

167

Dailies _____

May 17

"Give birth to your faith and you will always find yourself reborn. Life upon lifetime; soul upon self; one upon another."

—Robert

<u>168</u>

Day-To-Day Reminders _____

MAY 18

"A feather may flutter and flow randomly with the wind. Yet the wind is not random. The wind knows where the feather is being taken and when it will come to rest. Spirit is your wind and you are our feather, from the wing of the noblest of eagles. One feather among many traveling along a predestined path that was charted long before the eagle was brought forth by the Great Father."

– *The One Who Soars with Eagles*

Dailies _____

MAY 19

"Why choose to stall upon a path that is cleared? Why choose to hesitate in mid-flight? Why coast when you can soar? Allow the words—the thoughts—the inspiration—travel throughout your being. Would you be handed food if you were not meant to eat it? Let Spirit nourish your being as a meal nourishes your system. Stop picking over the meal before you and simply dig in! Eat! Enjoy! BE!"

– *The One Who Soars with Eagles*

MAY 20

"Sitting in the light doesn't necessarily blind you. It warms within as well as your outer suit—the one you willingly wear in this physical incarnation. Let the light illuminate you—your mind and spirit. Take it all within and let it nourish you."

– *The One Who Soars with Eagles*

Dailies _____

MAY 21

"There are always answers. Often times we just can't move beyond the question in order to see."

— *Thomas*

Day-To-Day Reminders _____

May 22

"Books are precious stones of wisdom. They provide glimpses into times gone by as well as glints of brilliance connecting yesterday, today and tomorrow. The words on the pages, however, never truly match the experiences of reading them for the very first time. What is written is read and what is read is shared. Pass the shining torch of knowledge on to the next curious mind and watch them brighten before your very soul!"

– Christopher

MAY 23

"No action IS an action. Sometimes no action is the action required. Other times it is merely an excuse. You are wondering how you can know the difference. That, little one, is where faith shines and blinds all doubt."

– The One Who Soars with Eagles

May 24

"Pride is much like a mighty, majestic Elk. Proud, magnificent, beautiful to behold but most dangerous and, for the most part, useless to take along on your journey."

— The One Who Soars with Eagles

Dailies _____

MAY 25

"Your words are still in infancy. They will mature in time. They will change over and over until they stand on their own. Like a proud parent you will watch them flourish! Do not permit your ego to snuff them out before they had a chance to run on their own!"

176 — The One Who Soars with Eagles

MAY 26

"As a child you had to crane your neck to look up to the adults, the sky, the trees, the table top. As the years passed you found you no longer had to do that. You are constantly growing. Like a flower reaching for the sun, bask in the warmth and love of the light and grow as high as only your own limitations will take you. Believe in limitless possibilities for then you will be soaring with the eagles."

—Robert

Dailies _____

MAY 27

"Insecurities are not truths. So why do you expend so much energy believing them to be?"

– The One Who Soars with Eagles

Day-To-Day Reminders _____

May 28

"What ARE you waiting for? Take the initiative. It is you who steps out onto the tundra to begin the passage. It is you who steps forward and into the light in order to cumulate a lifetime of dreams. And it is you who merely waits for anything other than yourself. Spirit can encourage and support. Spirit will not do what you are meant to do. Belly up to the bar—if it is your desire—and order what you want."

– Thomas

May 29

"The excitement within the limitless possibilities fuels the foraging steps of each and every journey. Walk the path with continuing enthrallment and fortitude of faith. While the faith will, from time to time, seem to falter, you must do your best to keep it. Hold it close and hold it dear. Keep the faith for it will keep you."

— Robert

MAY 30

"Trust yourself as you trust God. We are here—you know that. There is no need to question the obvious, is there? No. Then why do you dog paddle in the same spot? You are moving but not progressing! Wasted energy…merely wasted energy. Avoid the box altogether and bloom outside the conventional!"

— Robert

Dailies _____

MAY 31

"There is only 'one way' but the pathways leading there are infinite!"

— *Thomas*

June 1

"If you cannot speak the clarity—the truth—of your heart how can you expect us to hear it? Be honest with yourself first and the truth will be heard."

— Robert

Dailies _____

JUNE 2

"There are avenues to cross just as there are avenues to travel on. It's up to you to turn the corner."

– Robert

Day-To-Day Reminders _____

Dailies

JUNE 3

"Never dismiss the beauty of your own soul."

— Robert

Day-To-Day Reminders

Dailies _____

June 4

"There is a time when you have to accept who you are and what you do. We do not mean to overwhelm you. We mean to show our support, our belief, and know that our hands and our wings are at your back always. If you fall backwards we shall catch you. But YOU have to get up again."

— Robert

JUNE 5

"Live it. Be it. For it is within. For it is."

— The One Who Soars with Eagles

Dailies _____

JUNE 6

"Instead of trying to get one up on somebody else why don't you figure out why you're so down on yourself."

— Thomas

JUNE 7

"Do not doubt just because your time frame is not ours. Let faith fill the gaps between us so we are seamless."

— Robert

June 8

"Wisdom comes over time while unconditional love is instilled from the very beginning. Yet you spend so much time pursuing one and making the other so-very-conditional. Where's the wisdom in that, Oh-Great-Seeker?"

– Thomas

June 9

"The beauty within already resides there. But it's up to you to invite it out into the open. Live it! Be it!"

— Robert

Dailies _____

JUNE 10

"Love one another as you would love yourself. If you aren't doing the former then perhaps you should discover why you refuse to do the latter. Start from there."

– Thomas

June 11

"Be your own face value, the living embodiment of your word. Your actions are not merely a reflection of your intentions—they ARE part of you, no different than a limb or muscle. Every move, every reaction, every intention speaks volumes. Do your part to ensure that what you are saying is indeed what you want heard."

— The Collective

Dailies _____

JUNE 12

"Allow your spirit to soar into the wind of God's intent! Nurture your need as you would your child; lead it by the hand but allow it the freedom to explore the obvious curiosities along the way. Never cease asking questions for that is how you broaden your spirit, your mind, your body, your soul! Four elements, four directions, four archangels, all with One focal point!"

— Robert

Day-To-Day Reminders _____

June 13

"A blind man knows the sidewalk is before him without seeing it. He knows each step will be met with solid ground. It is time for you to embrace your faith and see as the blind man does: with your heart, eyes and faith as one."

— Robert

June 14

"One thing is never just that: one thing. One thing is, in reality, always many things! As no journey ever has only one destination, just as love can never be defined with one simplistic example, nor one individual is never one dimensional. One is ALL: a private personalized unique experience for each. Experience it on a singular level, feel it on a universal level!"

– Robert

June 15

"Is it truly better to be within a room with all of the objects you crave or within a life with all the love you want?"

— Robert

<u>197</u>

June 16

"Allow the light to reveal all facets of the jewel that is you. Do not dwell only on what you see—that which is in shadow must be inspected as well. That is only when you have full understanding: when all sides of the box are revealed!"

– Robert

June 17

"What you seek is already within your hand. You merely have to open your fingers to better see it. Set it free like a butterfly from its cocoon. Let the beauty soar for all to enjoy!"

— Robert

199

Dailies _____

June 18

"Remember your childhood dreams and embrace them. The earliest steps of your youth should never be forgotten in adulthood. For those baby steps brought you to where you stand today."

— Laura

June 19

"Do not allow your flame to be snuffed out by those who are not even worthy of lighting your candle in the first place."

— Thomas

Dailies _____

June 20

"Anyone can have an eye-opening experience. The hard part is keeping them open, especially in what you perceive to be darkness."

— Thomas

Day-To-Day Reminders _____

June 21

"Allow yourself the awareness of what is truly going on within you. We have a tendency of standing too close to the TV thus missing out on the big picture. Remember, boys and girls, life is in a letterbox format... it has NOT been formatted and cropped to fit your screen. If it HAS been then it's you who did it and only you can undo it. Stop existing. Start Living."

— *Thomas*

Dailies _____

JUNE 22

"Go with your instinct, for your instinct is us."

— Laura

Day-To-Day Reminders _____

June 23

"We embrace you as God embraces all of us. Within the white light, within the spiritual womb, for there you grow and you are nourished and you learn."

— Laura

June 24

"You are prompted from the very beginning to properly give thanks. How often did your parents remind you to say thank you for any acknowledgement or token you were given? The words THANK YOU—whether aloud or within the comfort of your own soul—are heaven sent. So is the seemingly simple act of accepting gratitude. To 'blow it off' is denying yourself the honor of some else's appreciation. If your kindness was 'no big deal' to you then what does that say of the significance of all parties involved? Thank you, my friends. Thank YOU."

— Joseph

June 25

"The truth that lies within the white light is visible and attainable. Watch how it glistens and dances before you. It is as real as a flame. Focus your energies on that and behold the brightness emitting from it."

— Robert

Dailies _____

JUNE 26

"Always keep the book open for each page will reveal to you more wondrous things. And your eyes will feast upon the lessons that unfold for you."

— Robert

Day-To-Day Reminders _____

June 27

"One true thing that stays constant is that love never abandons or never fades."

— Robert

June 28

"When you are a small child taking your first steps, you hold onto objects and people to steady yourself. In your spiritual infancy we are the ones you reach to in order to keep your balance. Like the loving parent, we will not let you hurt yourself. You may fall, from time to time, but we will be right there to pick you up and comfort you with the unconditional love that you need."

— Robert

June 29

"You never see your progress until you look where you have been. Never dwell on it. Keep your eye on the road ahead. The journey is only as long as the view you wish to see. As long, as short, as broad or as narrow as you wish. You have the opportunity to see beyond anything you have ever dreamed. Do you settle or do you take in all of God's Wonder? It is up to you."

— Robert

Dailies _____

June 30

"Every day there is something new to learn, to know, to feel, to love. It is an on-going learning process. Spiritually, physically, emotionally. It runs the whole gambit. Nothing should be glossed over, everything should be embraced. It is all part of the never-ending circle of life."

— Robert

Day-To-Day Reminders _____

July 1

"Love one another and don't cause any trouble. And, honestly, for two simple rules like that it seems to be a very difficult thing for mankind to do! We are constantly mystified at this. What is wrong with you people?"

— Martin

213

July 2

"When you lose someone grief is a normal reaction. But do not let the grief govern your heart or cloud your spirit. They want you to remember the good times and the things that you shared. Remember what you had with them and that you are blessed to have these people in your life! They do not want you to be sad. They want you to kick up your heels and just have a good time. That's the gist of it."

— Martin

July 3

"There is no reason for you, or anyone, to fear God. God loves you unconditionally and the idea of being afraid of One who loves you so much is rather absurd, don't you think?"

– Robert

215

Dailies _____

JULY 4

"You are never alone. Never. There are many who come and go, both physically and spiritually. Every encounter you have is designed for a reason. Some good, some bad. The key is learning from each of these to help you lead a better life. It is best to leave bitterness behind and face the sunrise rather than not."

— Robert

Day-To-Day Reminders _____

July 5

"Before any storm there is a calm. And after each storm there is a calm. Everything returns full circle. You begin in the spirit world, you return to the spirit world. You never leave home. As the storm builds outside you are safe within your home and your heart. And, within your heart, God lives and waits for you."

— Robert

July 6

"There are those who will tell you life happens. There is no plan, it is just random. This is not true. Everything happens for a reason and, through all the red tape, it boils down to one very simple thing: God is love. God doesn't hate anyone and, since you are a part of God, there is no reason for you to hate anyone, either. Embrace one another, embrace your lives."

— Robert

July 7

"A bridge is not instantaneously completed nor crossed. It is put together piece-by-piece, stone by stone. It is traversed in the same manner, one step at a time. Then and only then will you reach the destinations beyond. Your destiny is not just in the crossing, but in the building of it as well. Take the responsibility. Get your hands dirty—stop relying on other contractors to do the work for you."

– Robert

Dailies _____

JULY 8

"Sometimes it takes someone else's voice to remind us that our own is worth sharing. Perk up your inner ears so that your heart can listen! The truth—your truth—will always resonate within."

— Christopher

Day-To-Day Reminders _____

July 9

"Not everyone is on the same page of the same book at the same time. Give a little leniency. Show leniency toward others as well as yourself. Especially yourself, because this is where everything starts. This is where everything lives. This is where everything begins. As long as you hold yourself up to your own mirror everything else will follow suit."

— Oliver

July 10

"You are of the white light. You are of the like mind. So you know within your heart, within your soul, that there is so much more than the brief "time" that you have in the physical. Be aware of all that is around you as well as within you and soon you will forget to even look at the clock."

— Robert

July 11

"Share who you are for you are the ultimate gift. Do not feel you have to hide your flowers from the sunshine, otherwise they will never fully bloom."

— Laura

Dailies _____

July 12

"A light is instrumental in so many ways. It illuminates, it warms, it allows you to read, see and find your way. You are a light to others and, at the same time, others are a light to you. Everyone has something to offer. Use the light to your advantage and you can only glow brighter yourself."

– Robert

July 13

"The brevity of life is an illusion. The unending love within it is the reality."

– Robert

Dailies _____

July 14

"Many spend so much of their time pursuing their purpose. Their 'reason for being' so-to-speak. Truth be told, your only 'reason' IS 'being.' What you do within that 'time' is entirely up to you—use it wisely. Don't waste it looking for the nose on your face. Instead of searching for what makes you happy simply BE happy."

— Thomas

July 15

"There is no clock to watch but the one you keep winding."

— Robert

227

Dailies _____

JULY 16

"There are nights when life seems to make no sense what-so-ever. It is at those times when something greater than absolute sense of it all is given: acceptance. Acceptance of its direction. Acceptance of its purpose. Do not resist it. Let it envelop you so you can see it—feel it—from within."

— Oliver

Day-To-Day Reminders _____

July 17

"Why do you concern yourself with what others may think? This is merely an avoidance of doing the real work: controlling your OWN. It starts with you. Be your own example so that others will take your lead."

— Joseph

Dailies _____

July 18

"Be your own miracle. Today. Every day."

– Laura

<u>230</u>

Day-To-Day Reminders _____

July 19

"You become the person you are by experience, by lessons, by hopefully learning as you go. You know not to stick your finger into a hot flame, for example. But, alas, some do not learn so quickly. You become the person you are by what you choose to learn. This makes up the whole of who you are in the physical world. In the spirit world it is the accrual of all of your lives and all of your experiences. This is what makes you One."

– Robert

JULY 20

"Look beyond your own "wants" and focus on the "needs" of those you love. You will then discover the breathtaking beauty of your surroundings, as well as yourself, when the light emits from you rather than on you."

— Joseph

July 21

"Waking up is easy. Motivating yourself to take the first step can be overwhelming—which is expected. After all, change brings forth "newness." The unknown needs to be trusted—embrace it—KNOW it will carry you to where you need to be."

– Oliver

Dailies _____

JULY 22

"Living a life in gratitude is wasted if you will not include yourself in the process. Be the embodiment of your own appreciation."

— The One Who Soars with Eagles

234

Day-To-Day Reminders _____

July 23

"People often confuse 'simplicity' with 'ease.' Devices are marketed with the alluring tag-line promising its purchase will simplify your life. All it really does is present yet another distraction. You want proof? How 'bout this: Your soul never needs an upgrade."

— Thomas <u>235</u>

July 24

"Birth and death are both transitions. Briefly leaving one reality behind in order to learn and experience another. You bounce back and forth—learning, enhancing, combining the two—in order to progress forward. You do not live for only yourself. You also live for the collective! Your daily inquiry is not only 'What am I learning?' but also 'What am I teaching?'"

— Oliver

July 25

"Look beyond the reasoning of today in order to believe in the infinite possibilities of tomorrow."

— Laura

July 26

"Do not make a promise to any Being other than yourself. Honesty begins, resides and blossoms only within your very essence. Denying yourself the luxury of your own promises is blasphemous in every concept of the definition. When one continually lies to oneself—building one lie upon another—how can your very existence be trusted, let alone your word?"

— Robert

July 27

"Be truthful with yourself—especially in your thoughts for that is where your physical reality begins and is stored."

— Robert

Dailies _____

JULY 28

"It isn't about listening, you know? It's about hearing and then applying what is heard into positive energetic action. So, are you going to sit there, turning a deaf soul to the source, or are you going to...? It's up to you."

— Thomas

Day-To-Day Reminders _____

July 29

"What is the purpose of building a bridge when your focus is on the "impassibility" of the actual crossing? One stone at a time, one step at a time, then GO!"

— Robert

Dailies _____

JULY 30

"Not every seed blooms but you won't know until you plant it."

— Robert

July 31

"Just because you do not understand something does not diminish its significance. Do not focus on what you *can* learn. Instead, actively participate in your own life in order to discover what you *will* learn!"

— Oliver

243

Dailies _____

AUGUST 1

"You are the definitive symbol of your own word. Honor them both."

– The One Who Soars with Eagles

Day-To-Day Reminders _____

AUGUST 2

"The speed means nothing. It is the understanding of each step that matters. Why is it taken? Is it solid and firm or loose and unsure? Truth is always unyielding and steadfast. The loose ground gives only unsure footing, unstable belief systems, vague views. All of these will crumble in the wind of change and tribulation. If ONE step is not true to your pace then do not take it. Walk within your own heart and only then can you ask the questions you must and receive the only answer you require."

– Robert

AUGUST 3

"You do not have to explain your wants and desires. Merely know what you want. Your intent will be the 'soul' reason. State to us what you desire with no limitations. Open all doors of possibilities. Leave nothing to 'chance.'"

— Robert

August 4

"Stand before yourself with the Knowing Honesty you give to others."

— Oliver

Dailies _____

AUGUST 5

"Cease asking 'why.' Accept it is for your best and highest and allow the petals within you to burst open so the great garden within you will bloom!"

— The One Who Soars with Eagles

Day-To-Day Reminders _____

AUGUST 6

"Love and understanding often times get misplaced along your journey. As spiritual beings we need to put much of our intent in both. Love is understanding without judgment. Understanding is love without question. It is 'acceptance' which bonds them together. Accept the love within as well as around and you will understand the no longer elusive 'why' of it all."

— The One Who Soars with Eagles

AUGUST 7

"It all begins here and it always returns to the point of origin! No matter what path you take, no matter the route you follow, in time you return home. You do not 'find your way' home as that implies you have been lost. It is as if you have merely gone to market to gather supplies of necessity and then returned home, returning from hence you came, reuniting with All that Is once more."

– The One Who Soars with Eagles

AUGUST 8

"The flow of Spirit—of the truth we convey—is expertly applied as an artist paints a canvas. It is to be not only enjoyed but to serve as a window of thoughts, emotions, universal understanding and realization. It strikes each recipient differently. Some interpret quickly while others dwell. The swiftness matters not. It is the application of the brush in the first place that truly matters."

– Oliver

AUGUST 9

"It is not just 'God's Plan,' you know? You are an equal partner in the design and completion. You ARE divine—never forget that, my child!"

– Laura

August 10

"Walk in the midst of your thoughts in order to truly understand the impact they have on your surroundings. For what you are comes from your intention of creation."

— Robert

AUGUST 11

"Be true to your speech. The truth – your truth – lies within the book within you. If you write it therefore you must live it."

– Christopher

August 12

"Open your ears in order to see. Open minds open revelations. Closed hearts deaden the light. Open! Open! Flowers instinctively reach for the light—no questions asked. You must do the same. The doubt clears—the fog of the conscious mind—once belief has taken root and begins to reach for the sun!"

—Robert

Dailies _____

AUGUST 13

"The speaking of the mind often inhibits the speaking of the soul. One has to wonder how this happened in the first place. Is it what you choose to hear? Or how you choose to listen?"

— *The One Who Soars with Eagles*

Day-To-Day Reminders _____

August 14

"Time changes all things: surroundings, perceptions, even memories. It is even said that time heals all wounds. But, in truth, is it not your heart that forgives? The passing of time can add maturity, clarity, understanding… but it cannot FEEL. Adjust your spiritual clock so forgiveness is at the top of the hour and not only acknowledged after hitting the snooze button one too many times. Wake up NOW—not later—so you won't miss a thing."

– Thomas

Dailies _____

AUGUST 15

"The depth and strength of the root is just as vital as the span of the branches. Maintain the balance within your own nature."

– The One Who Soars with Eagles

AUGUST 16

"Before you lies all: possibilities, prospects, defeats, challenges—every conceivable pro and con that your given imagination can manifest into what you call reality. This, my friend, is where many falter. You allow yourself to get caught up in the validity of perception and forgetting the actual truth. Yes, life can be hard, but must you become hardened as well? Compassion is the key that can open any door no matter how tightly it is shut. Keep your doors open allowing your light to shine forward, illuminating your own path. Those who opt not to see it—to bask within the warmth of it—do so of their own choice. Your obligation ends once the path is lit. You can merely show the way... not by pointing but by living the example."

—Robert

AUGUST 17

"In times of trouble there is no doubt. It is created within. It can be dismissed within."

— Joseph

AUGUST 18

"You cannot preach from a book for a book knows not. You preach from the heart for the heart knows all."

— Robert

AUGUST 19

"Where do you begin? At the beginning, of course. This is where the seed is planted. This is where the seed will grow. This is where the tree will sprout, where the flower will blossom. It has to come from that one singular point, that beginning of life. The life is the faith and the faith is what you believe, what you know is real within your heart. You cannot be impassioned about something you do not believe in. Especially yourself."

—Thomas

AUGUST 20

"Stretch across the seemingly endless borders of your own faith and you will discover a vast, uncharted territory that will, despite the untrodden ground, still feel oh-so-very familiar."

– Robert

August 21

"When you shake a tree at its base, fresh fruit is dislodged. It falls to the ground surrounding you. But the tree shall not fall for the roots are deeply encased in Your Mother Earth. The foundation, like yours, is strong. Stronger than you sometimes realize or remember. The only way this tree can fall is if YOU cut it down. Your faith is that tree. You are in charge of its power as well as its durability."

— Robert

AUGUST 22

"New Found Love, in reality, has always been right there, awaiting your own breath of life to be given. You must bring it forth in order to see yourself in truth. You can lie to yourself all you want. But once the soul—the true soul—sees the first rays of your sun it can no longer lie dormant. Cultivate your soul garden for it IS yours."

— Robert

Dailies _____

AUGUST 23

"All imprints leave a mark. What do yours say about you? Do they form a path to be followed? What are the remnants left behind? Yes, all imprints leave a mark. Make sure they are indelible and as credible as you."

— Oliver

AUGUST 24

"Doubt can loom over you, can't it? This is not always a bad thing. Doubt can provide you a chance to think things through. It can, at times, lead you to more clarity, true understanding. The intimidating shadow, like that of the tallest tree on an eerie moonlit night, provides only temporary and unsure protection. The key here, my friends, is to make sure you do not take up permanent residence within that short-term shelter. Do not forget the darkness dissipates with the resurgence of the sun. Remember to step out from the shadowy confines into the light of The Creator. Your light. There's no sense in wasting a beautiful day, now is there?"

— Thomas

Dailies _____

AUGUST 25

"You must participate within your own life. The steps must be taken by you, one before the other, setting your own rhythm and pace. Relying on others for motivation or inspiration, instead of sensing your own, will throw you off your beat placing you out of step. If there is a knock at your door you must take the steps to open it or not. Either is fine. Waiting for—or worse yet—*expecting* someone else to take your role only ensures the ineffectiveness of your once distinct cadence. Step up! Step up and refuse to allow yourself to take 'NO' as a self-inflicted sentence."

— Robert

AUGUST 26

"It is not always about learning. More times than not it is about teaching. What lessons are you teaching? What lessons are you living?"

– Oliver

Dailies _____

AUGUST 27

"Until you reach the summit you never really grasp the view. If you think what you are seeing now is breathtaking then just wait until you ascend to the next level."

– Laura

<u>270</u>

Day-To-Day Reminders _____

AUGUST 28

"There is always time for change. There is always time for growth, forgiveness. But do not waste the time given. Do it and move on."

– Oliver

August 29

"Open your eyes and watch the flame. Remember the truth is always within the light. It dances with the wind and it can even extinguish. But it can always be relit. The key is to never let the flame go out. However, when it does, you have the power to light it once again and continue dispelling the darkness."

— Robert

AUGUST 30

"God lays a map before you. It is always clear once you have unfolded it to its entirety. Do not let any flaps hide part of your path from your view. Once you see your full destination your journey will be much easier. You will find obstacles—you will learn from them for that is why they are there. Know all lessons lead to a final ceremony of commencement. Follow the light for it will always be high above showing the way to the next class and the one after that. You are given the books. You are given the maps. But it is you who must open them. Class is in session…"

— Robert

AUGUST 31

"A lighthouse is a beacon to lost ships and will guide them to safety only when the lamp is lit and bright. You are your own lighthouse keeper. You must keep the lamp polished so the light will shine through the darkest of storms with the brightness of truth spreading to all those about you, yourself included. Polish the lamp so you may see your own wondrous reflection gazing back. The truth is in your eyes just as it is within YOUR light. Will you let it shine or will you douse it out?"

– Robert

SEPTEMBER 1

"You close the doors behind you without looking back in order to step into the empty hallway ahead… The Mansion's corridors await your footsteps. There is no need to walk softly and cautiously. You have chosen the padding beneath your feet so step on it with firm confidence. Leave your mark! Not to serve as a map backwards but to remind you of the depth of your own steps of self-assured conviction."

275

— Robert

September 2

"Compassion is an automatic reaction. Thinking, on the other hand, is merely an excuse to dismiss what comes naturally."

— Laura

SEPTEMBER 3

"There is more to life than just 'finding your peace.' You must, at the onset, maintain your peace, share your peace and, most importantly, BE your peace. Be by example in order to cast the most solid of reflections."

— Robert

Dailies _____

SEPTEMBER 4

"Seek within, share throughout."

– Christopher

Day-To-Day Reminders _____

SEPTEMBER 5

"An adjustment in your 'altitude' brings you heightened clarity. Rise above eye-level in order to see both the horizon of tomorrow as well as reflecting on the beauty of yesterday. Remember, even the clouds casting seemingly dark shadows are all part of the Master's plan. No speck of the territory is unknown to the Creator—nor should it be unappreciated by you. This IS my country: your own terrain. Care for it in order for it to best care for you."

— *The One Who Soars with Eagles*

September 6

"Speak from your heart, not your mouth. Pray throughout your soul, not within your mind. Live inside your truth, not just your house. Embrace the reality of your faith, release the illusion of control. Believe and it shall be."

— Laura

SEPTEMBER 7

"Too many are busy plugging in when they need to be tuning in. What you classify as 'entertainment' is nothing more than another distraction, an excuse. Tap to the beat of your own soul. Let it sound above all else. Feel the distinctive rhythm within and throughout. Keep in step on all of the paths along the way—yours as well as those you are blessed to cross. Once you fully feel the ticking of your own metronome you will be able to sense the ripple effect of your soul waves on all levels. Now THAT is music! Music of the mind, the heart and the spirit."

— Joseph

SEPTEMBER 8

"How you wish to be perceived is not always how others perceive you. You may lament that 'no one truly knows me!' The stark light of reality often reveals just the opposite. Gaze honestly into the mirror and take in the reflection before you, with eyes and mind wide open, and note what you are…to yourself as well as to others. Make sure that you can, without hesitancy, meet that gaze in personal and Universal love."

– Pamela

SEPTEMBER 9

"Nothing is sadder than blank pages left untended. Fill them with your thoughts, your prayers, your hopes for all of these things—and more—make up your life. The very life you are writing along with the Ultimate Collaborator."

– Christopher

SEPTEMBER 10

"What is the point of buying a book if you are only going to keep it out of reach high upon a shelf? It must be read. It must be utilized. Its purpose must brought forth in order to fulfill its reason for being written. Why have you been written? You must live your manuscript, without skipping to the end, to find out. Always keep the book open in the light for each page will reveal to you more wondrous things."

— Christopher

SEPTEMBER 11

"So many times we forget to let our loved ones know what they mean to us; how we cherish them in our lives and the fact their voice can be as sacred to us as their touch. Do not let a lifetime pass between exchanges. Cherish those you love and make sure they know it. And, never, under any circumstance, lose your humanity. God Bless the World. No Exceptions."

— The Collective

Dailies _____

SEPTEMBER 12

"Love is, like you, constantly changing, yet permanent."

— Laura

SEPTEMBER 13

"Healing. That lone word can conjure up many connotations, does it not? It is multi-layered as well as faceted. As a diamond has brilliance reflecting from each side, the gem does not look the same from any two angles. Each view presents a unique perspective—each one as breathtaking as the next. Looking at a jewel of beauty is no different than fully understanding a word—or process—such as 'healing'. What form of healing do you seek? What do you require? This must be understood within your very being—your soul stamp—in order to get the most from the process. To speak your mind IS to speak your soul's wants and needs!"

—Robert

Dailies _____

SEPTEMBER 14

"Healing IS a process. A process of mind, body and spirit! Each can be inflicted with what you would call dis-ease. Each level—each dimension of you—should be treated equally yet in a different way. To better know and value oneself requires at first an acknowledgment of each separate piece. You are the sum of all parts of God, of the Universe, of yourself! WHAT DO YOU WANT? Do not fear specifics for it is YOUR life!"

– Robert

SEPTEMBER 15

"Within the Ark of the Covenant lie great secrets. Within the heart of Man lies just as many. Be advised the secrets, when used improperly, can be disastrous. But when used in the proper way the beauty will unfold like flowers on a spring day soaking up the sun that is your Spirit, feeding on the rain of tears as well as the brightness of all joy and love. You must care for the secrets. Each soul carries different ones within them. Each speaks louder than their ancestors and is brighter than a thousand suns enlightening the way for future generations. The light of the truth, of the soul, cannot be extinguished nor will it ever dim. Providing, of course, that you never turn it out. It is up to you."

– Christopher

SEPTEMBER 16

"There are those who mock, who ridicule, who aggravate. They generally apply their trade on those within the light. It is not maliciousness. It is fear. They do not fully understand so they fight back. See it from their point of view. You may not agree with it but you CAN understand it. An infant does not know any better so they must be taught. Teach those infants you encounter along your path and all will be enriched."

– Oliver

SEPTEMBER 17

"Quiet yourself. Right now. Take a moment—just one of the precious ones you are given—and just be *still*. Allow your mind to drift like the early morning mist throughout your body. Breathe the sun and stars into your very essence. Fill your physical form with the wonders of the Universe. Open the gates of stillness in order for this Universal Power to merge with your Spirit. Listen to what the silence has to teach. Permit yourself this brief retreat from all distractions... some valid and some self-inflicted. Silence your inner discomforts and by dealing with them within your own calm for that is where YOU truly reside. The simplicity of your core being. Still the external, pray with the internal, live in both with better clarity. Quiet yourself..."

– *The One Who Soars with Eagles*

SEPTEMBER 18

"In step, one at a time, one after another, again and again and again. It may appear repetitious but that is only how it shall seem on the outside looking in. How often have you been incorrect in your judgments? Too many times you have gazed upon a subject and decided upon the validity of facts that are anything but factual. Taking one step after another, over and over and over, is anything but routine. Each step is unique. Each imprint left behind has a purpose as well as a depth. Acknowledge all steps made for all have made you."

– Robert

SEPTEMBER 19

"Routine—the mundane lack of feeling—comes once the driven passion within your intentions has been silenced. Stop finding ways to forget what steps need to be taken, what stages must be reached. Rediscover what you have known from the beginning and stop dismissing the footprints of others. What if they begin to dismiss yours? Truly an epidemic of catastrophic proportions, would you not agree? Keep IN step with yourself and with others within all Light."

— Robert

September 20

"Implement what you have learned. Place it into action and reaction at every opportunity. What is the point of having a glorious treasure if it cannot be seen, utilized and shared? Greed of the heartless will insist you hoard it. Emotionless trickery will convince you to keep it under a fear-based lock and key. Do not listen. Do NOT listen. When your treasure is kept within the dark place no one, yourself included, can benefit or enjoy the once brilliant reflections. If the rays of the Light cannot shine upon you they most certainly cannot reflect."

— Robert & Oliver

SEPTEMBER 21

"What ignites the flame within? Does it burn to life as an action or a reaction? A fire cannot be lit until that initial spark. The smallest burst of light can bring forth a consuming inferno. The blaze can clear a path or destroy it. Will you direct it? Or will you permit it to go out of control?"

– Joseph **295**

SEPTEMBER 22

"Do not allow yourself to be bogged down by your past. Have no regrets for everything you have done and have gone through, endured, has brought you to where you are, who you are and why you are. It is all meant to be."

— Robert

SEPTEMBER 23

"You cannot take the hand of another without extending yours as well. In order to be a part *of* the chain—the link—you must take part *in* the chain."

— *Pamela*

SEPTEMBER 24

"The mist is always frustrating at first but remember it is only fleeting. In time it passes and the road before you is once again clear."

— Pamela

SEPTEMBER 25

"Being alive encompasses so many things. It takes on much responsibility. Embrace all of it. Do not discard pieces to suit your fancy. Embrace it all, live it all and this will enable you to understand it. Not necessarily here, on the physical plane, but in the spiritual plane it will come together. Trust will lead you, so follow."

— Martin

SEPTEMBER 26

"On your shelves you have many objects. Some are functional. Some are decorative. Some are sentimental. All are essential for diverse reasons therefore all are necessary. Spirituality, as well as life, is the same. There are many aspects; there are many singular parts, all of them vital. None of them are unnecessary. Merely arrange them so that they best suit you as well. Clutter is one thing but functional clutter is something else entirely. Arrange your life so that it best suits your path. Do not try to fit a path through your life. Don't make the pieces fit. Simply FIND the pieces that fit. You will know."

— Robert

September 27

"The issue is not necessarily feeling lost or without direction. It is, in reality, about questioning your own bearing. Keep in mind that 'dormancy' IS a 'direction.' This is often unseen. Honestly answer this, my child, *Where do I want to go?'* Pull the magnet away from the compass and allow it to work, to flow, to point without influence."

— Pamela

Dailies _____

SEPTEMBER 28

"Have you ever noticed the self-proclaimed 'realists' are anything but? A distorted perception is the cornerstone of a foundation destined to crumble. Negativity builds nothing. It is the sturdy steel of truth that will enable you—your words, your actions—to stand tall and rise to the heavens."

— *Christopher*

September 29

"You ARE part of the greater good. To think otherwise is a blatant slap in your own face. The omission of love, especially self-love, leaves behind a hole that cannot be filled until you understand why it was dug in the first place."

— Thomas

<u>303</u>

September 30

"Playin' don't mean you're wastin' time. It shows n' shares how ya celebrate life!"

— Dondi

OCTOBER 1

"Even on the warmest summer day one is aware of the approaching winter. Prepare for what is ahead, but do not ignore the vitality of this day."

— Robert

305

October 2

"Open lungs, open eyes, open mind, open heart, open soul. Everything must be open. The locks cannot be twisted shut for everything to pass through. The doors must be open. Even one locked lock will impede your speed and your progress. You have the keys. You are the locksmith. How fast do you want to go? How fast do YOU want to go?"

— Christopher

OCTOBER 3

"Greatness does not come in the shiny wrapping of grandeur or in the spot light of the world stage. It is merely there, masked from attention, yet plainly in view. It is recognized by the soul as truth because it IS truth. Love and positive intent made the step in order for the truth to remain. What steps are you taking to ensure that what you leave behind is a truly beautiful imprint of what you believe?"

– Robert

Dailies _____

OCTOBER 4

"Gratitude is not an expression; it is a state of being, of living. True gratitude exudes from the heart instinctively without thought. It IS an honest reaction to the Love you have just received."

— Robert

OCTOBER 5

"Live and learn. How many times have you heard that? And how often have you really thought about its validity? You live, you learn. You live to learn and you learn to live. At least we hope so. All those lessons you've picked up along the way? How many do you share? Do not keep them to yourself. Share with the class. Share the benefits, reap the rewards, so others will learn and live by example, not rhetoric."

– Oliver & Thomas

Dailies _____

OCTOBER 6

"A spider sits in the middle of its web, still, centered and perfectly aware of its environment. The slightest vibration alerts it to advance, retreat or, when the situation warrants, to sit perfectly still. Are you, like the spider, aware of your own surroundings? Do you comprehend the effect each can have on you? Or are you confusing being in the center of your web with being the center of your own isolated universe?"

– *The One Who Soars with Eagles*

OCTOBER 7

"When shopping you will normally find yourself selecting your favorite brands. It's habit. It's what you're used to doing. Maybe you're buying it because it's what your grandmother used. It's what you were taught. Or perchance you were taken in by an advertisement. Your decision, conscious or not, does stem from a reason. Everything does. Attitude, behavior, traditions, prides & prejudices, actions & reactions. You choose each one and check it off your shopping list. Then, one day you realize Brand X just doesn't tackle grass stains like it used to. It no longer serves. So it's time for a change. Trade the negative for a positive. Rethink your reasons. If they are unreasonable it may be time to switch brands itself. It's never too late for something new & improved."

— Thomas

Dailies _____

OCTOBER 8

"Gratitude is just as significant and moving as the gift itself, if not more so. Do not permit yourself to miss out on sharing both."

– Robert

<u>312</u>

OCTOBER 9

"Like water, there is a flow to life. Depending on the terrain, seen and unseen, you will flow with the current or resist the ease of it. You will ride high on the crest of the swells or dip below the waves only to break through to the surface once more. The common element is constant movement. From the most tumultuous of storms to the gentle natural flow, you ARE moving. It is those times, when you cannot see even the slightest of ripples, that your action is the most vital. In what you think is dormancy is in fact the time when you must faithfully tread water to stay afloat. Life is movement. Life is participation. Life is interaction. Tread when you must, float when you can, and know you are swimming safely with us along your river of life!"

— The One Who Soars with Eagles

October 10

"A child sees truth. And when the child expresses their clarity they are accused of lying by the adult. So, in turn, the elder teaches the child another lie and another and another. This is done until the flame of fact is shrouded within ignorant darkness, the false truth. But somewhere, deep within the grown child resides a memory, a lone burning ember of actuality. And sometimes, when exposed to the right circumstances, with the right people, that fire ignites once more. You began with the light of truth and now you must use your torch to relight the furnace within the homes that have, temporarily, gone dark. And all are grateful."

— Robert

OCTOBER 11

"Insight is intuition. You know, on an energetic level, a spiritual level, what is needed, what is missing, what is. And how many times do you 'convince' yourself that it is all in your head? That it is 'wrong' and cannot be trusted? What evidence do you require? Time and time again you see examples of what is and what is not and yet… you dismiss it. How long do you wish to live in darkness all the while having an infinite supply of matches right at your fingertips?"

– Robert

October 12

"What do you hear when you have no distractions? Do you permit yourself to be comfortable within your own silence? Why do you convince yourself the sunset on television is more beautiful than the one right outside your very window? Appreciate what IS. Experience it up-close and personal. Use YOUR senses not those electronic falsities. Allow it all in. Embrace the reality of sensory overload and see how quickly the clarity comes along for the ride."

— Thomas

October 13

"Don't be selective when it comes to your blessings."

— Joseph

Dailies _____

OCTOBER 14

"Spend your time walking, not watching. Pledge your time giving from your heart, not taking from others. Use your time taking part, not partly living. Share what you have, share in what is given."

— Laura

318

OCTOBER 15

"Your religion matters not. Your faith matters most."

– Christopher

OCTOBER 16

"What you seek is not always attainable. Does this mean you should stop trying? What would life be without goals? A great artist is not focused on the final masterpiece. No. They are enthralled, educated, enticed by each and every brush stroke. The discovery of something new, whether it is a technique or merely a point of view, cannot be rivaled. Sometimes it is best to change mediums in mid-stroke. Constant rediscovery enables constant realizations. About yourself, about others, about life—all life."

– Robert

OCTOBER 17

"As long as you reach out there will always be something to grasp. You are never empty-handed."

— Oliver

321

Dailies _____

OCTOBER 18

"The goals you have set for yourself within the confines of your own soul are the advances that truly matter."

– Robert

<u>322</u>

Day-To-Day Reminders _____

OCTOBER 19

"A quilt is designed with great care and thought. It is strategically stitched together one piece at a time. Ultimately, it will unfold before you and the tapestry will make sense in its entirety. Until then, enjoy each new section of fabric as it is revealed to you. You spend far too much time wondering what the next piece will be rather than appreciating the one you are currently seeing."

— Laura

October 20

"Practice what you are taught. There is no need to have an equation on the chalkboard before you if you have no intention of completing it. You have the chalk and, yes, the eraser. Now you need the answer. The answer is right before your eyes. You need to open your eyes and see it, understand it, and believe it. Believe in it, believe in yourself, believe in your own ability to solve it. It is all based on belief. Believe in God as God believes in You."

– Oliver

_____ *Dailies*

OCTOBER 21

"You must not limit yourself to just one form of ideal exchange."

— *Robert*

<u>325</u>

_____ *Day-To-Day Reminders*

OCTOBER 22

"You must unclog your quill. Clean your quill so the penmanship of your life's book will flow smoothly onto the porous parchment and therefore be easily consumed by the hungry eyes of those willing and eager to learn. Your actions glorify the words of your intent and they will all meld into one ball. A ball that is easily tossed from one individual to the next. A game of spiritual 'catch' for an unlimited number of most willing participants."

– Christopher

OCTOBER 23

"There is a season for planting, there is a season for harvesting. Ergo, one cannot expect to benefit from the crops before they are placed in the ground, correct? There is a rhyme and a reason for all things. You must strive for patience and simplistic faith. Believe in your ability to do so and all will come to you in its time."

327

— Laura

OCTOBER 24

"Development, progression, evolution are constant. Each sunrise shines light upon new opportunities, new lessons learned as well as taught. Be at the ready. Keep preparing just as an Olympic runner prepares for a race. Be ready and open your heart, mind and spirit and you will reach the finish line in record time."

— Robert

October 25

"Prayer is a strong weapon and will always come out triumphant. Perhaps not in the physical world but in the spiritual realm it will. This is a difficult notion to grasp with the physical mind but so easily comprehendible within your faith. You must remember your physical life is intertwined within your spiritual. Both are on-going, separate yet seamless, entwined together creating the strongest of bonds."

— Robert

Dailies _____

OCTOBER 26

"Stop focusing on 'what if' and start focusing on 'what is' in order to manifest what will be."

— Martin

Day-To-Day Reminders _____

OCTOBER 27

"Perception can make or break a day. It is entirely up to you. If you knock over cans of paint do you focus on the mess or the rainbow spreading before you?"

– Thomas

Dailies _____

OCTOBER 28

"Own the space within instead of the space you take up."

— *Thomas*

332

Day-To-Day Reminders _____

OCTOBER 29

"Seek answers within your heart not your mind. The key to spirituality is to not think but go with instinct. Go with what your heart tells you for the heart is where the love of *all* is stored. The heart is the key to physical existence, God is the key to all existence. The heart symbolizes love, God IS love. Hand in hand, heart in heart, all acting as one." <u>**333**</u>

— Robert

October 30

"Your spirit is a multi-faceted diamond. There are so many sides to it. No matter how the light shines upon the many surfaces they still sparkle, they still glisten, and they are still beautiful to the eye. The light obliterates the flaws from view. Sure, the cracks and chips are still there but they just don't matter. The beauty blinds you and allows you, and others, to bask in your warm glow. Share your light."

— Martin

OCTOBER 31

"Greatness comes in all forms in multiple ways. You do not have to go out and save the world in order to achieve it. Just spread the joy, the news, the information. One simple sentence passed on to another can give much needed food for thought or satisfy the thirst of one who craves peace of mind, of spirit. Greatness provides the nutrients as you cater the ultimate feast." **335**

— Martin & Robert

Dailies _____

NOVEMBER 1

"You can cross a river in many ways: a bridge, stones, or swim. It is best to know where the stones are before you step. This is where your faith comes in. Believe they are there and they will be."

— Robert

NOVEMBER 2

"Memories are the scrapbook of the soul. Preserve them for future seekers who come along the way."

— Joseph

NOVEMBER 3

"Life is a very complex thing. It is not just merely the beating of a heart, the passing of blood through veins. Life is everything you experience along the way. Your experiences store within you and the vibration, the energy, the essence of these experiences are not only with you but they come out! When you meet someone you can sense if they are angry or sad, or a good person or bad person. Each day, each moment, you have a decision to make. Do you want to share the negative or the positive? Do you want to dine on good food or bad? Serve up what you would eat and watch your table fill with the most bountiful of things!"

— Martin

NOVEMBER 4

"It is important that you ask the questions that are on your mind as well as merely tuning in for the experience of it all. Sometimes you need to drive. Other times you need to ride along in the passenger's seat in order to see."

– Robert

<u>339</u>

NOVEMBER 5

"Loss is a part of life. I am sure you have heard that expression many times over. And, I am equally assured, that you have come to know and understand it as truth. There is pain and sadness associated with loss. But what you sometimes fail to realize is what of the loss of never having the experience in the first place? A loved one passes from the physical and you feel the loss, the sadness. But they leave behind so many memories. If you never had this loved one in your life at all then what would you have? Nothing. And THAT is a true loss. Work through the sadness but keep the joy and know you never lose those you love."

– Robert

NOVEMBER 6

"Your prayers are felt. Your prayers are heard. Not only by the Creator but by those you are praying for, you understand? Your prayers are part of your life-force, the will of your heart, the purity of your intent. What may only take a moment to utter can extend for a duration beyond your physical comprehension. Prayer covers the distance just as the stars cover the evening sky or as a mother covers her child at night. Infinite love in its strongest and purest of forms."

– Martin

NOVEMBER 7

"Catch your own light while it is moving. Hold it but a moment—a fleeting caress if you will—and send it back on its intended way. Your light must circulate. It must flow in order for it, and you, to forge its way leaving its intended mark. It always returns for your touch for you are its source as well as its vessel. Your light comes from you, through you and back to you while touching so many along the way. So very many."

— Christopher

NOVEMBER 8

"You grow throughout life. Some by leaps and bounds and others, well, not so much. When something annoys you it's often because you have distanced yourself from that sort of thing spiritually, energetically. It's no longer a part of your life-force. It's not a piece of your reality. You've risen above such things. This does not imply that you are coming from a place of ego; it's simply an issue of clarity, a matter of fact. When you have that understanding it is so much easier to get through the maze. You already know where to turn. Deep within, you know. Sometimes you will have to make those turns on your own. But there's always something new around the next turn. You're not leaving anything behind. You're gaining. You're growing. Just turn the corner and see what's there."

— Thomas

November 9

"Would you willingly bear a cauldron of boiling oil? It would be the equivalent of carrying harsh pain with you no matter where you travel. It would be burdensome and counterproductive, thus slowing and weakening your every step. It would begin to alter, then dominate and ultimately destroy your journey. With that in mind, why would you willingly carry a grudge? Release the burden and leave your hands free to truly receive the love you are missing."

— Robert

NOVEMBER 10

"Forgiveness is your 'get out of jail free' card but without the exertion of tossing the dice. Don't just sit there…use it."

— Thomas

Dailies _____

NOVEMBER 11

"The seed of Forgiveness is planted within your heart—your core—at your inception. It is your responsibility to properly tend to your garden. Care for it, nourish it. It is within your hands, your control, that dictates whether the seeds will flourish or whither. Which shall it be?"

— Joseph

November 12

"Actions and words work as one. One thought, one intent, one soul. They serve as a reflection of you. Do all you can to ensure this is a reflection you can face in the mirror each morn."

— Robert

347

Dailies _____

NOVEMBER 13

"Far too many are, more often than not, more concerned about what is going in their mouths rather that what comes out."

— Thomas

<u>348</u>

Day-To-Day Reminders _____

November 14

"Before you pledge to 'walk the walk' make sure you understand why you're taking the steps in the first place."

— Oliver

Dailies _____

NOVEMBER 15

"There is a profound wisdom within each of us. When spoken—when practiced—it will often fall upon deaf ears. Do not permit the selective deafness of others to worry you. Your only concern should be making sure you have not lost your own hearing as well."

– The One Who Soars with Eagles

November 16

"It is not the crowd that sits before you that is important, but your integrity as you stand before them."

– Robert

Dailies _____

NOVEMBER 17

"What is, is. What was, was. What will be is in the making. Always in the making."

— *The One Who Soars with Eagles*

<u>352</u>

Day-To-Day Reminders _____

November 18

"Refrain from looking back over your shoulder. Live in the moment. All the while having faith in the direction of the road ahead."

– Martin

Dailies _____

NOVEMBER 19

"You cannot expect to solve the equations on the board before you without taking part in the entire class. The answers you seek come not from skipping a grade but through thorough understanding, awareness and the simplest of faith."

— Oliver

Day-To-Day Reminders _____

NOVEMBER 20

"The door is shut on yesterday in order to open the window to tomorrow. Enjoy the view."

— Joseph

Dailies _____

NOVEMBER 21

"Your step, like your word, should be true and not misleading, assured but not arrogant, firm but not destructive. It matters not whether you lead or follow, speak aloud or only to one's self. All are equally powerful and it is you, and you alone, who controls the strength and drive behind it all."

— The One Who Soars with Eagles

NOVEMBER 22

"Watch where you are going, remember where you have been, always live in the now. Today will give you the wisdom to understand the occurrences of yesterday as well as the enthusiasm to envision tomorrow."

– Joseph

357

Dailies _____

NOVEMBER 23

"How you see stems from your own self-perception."

– Robert

NOVEMBER 24

"Budget your time wisely and truthfully. Would you prefer to waste your time imagining what you cannot do or spend your time sharing what you can?"

— Christopher

Dailies _____

November 25

"An award on your shelf may look nice, but it is the reward of yourself that surpasses all accolades."

– Robert

Day-To-Day Reminders _____

November 26

"Take stock in what surrounds you. I am not referencing the staples—family, home, neighbors. I am calling your attention to the rest. What you may consider "the little things." Take the time to appreciate the well choreographed randomness of what dances throughout your day-to-day. As you live to the music of the Soul, your eyes will open. You will discover inspiration where you once saw coincidence, comfort where once was a fleeting glance, hope in the place of a dismissed shrug. Once these signs are seen and felt you can finally take your place on the dance floor serving as a sign to another Spirit on the brink of their own awakening."

— Robert & Pamela

NOVEMBER 27

"Gaze upon the terrain as you soar overhead. There are many roadways crisscrossing the terracotta beneath you. Each connecting destination to destination, each singularly created to serve many over time. Each is purposeful from the initial conception. A few grow over in time and seem impassible to some. Until an explorer, one of an inquisitive mind and spirit, foresees its use once more. An explorer who clears the path for other to follow or, more importantly, to widen the consciousness of the next generation of wanderers. As you walk your path ask yourself for whom you are clearing the way. And how will it appear from upon high."

— The One Who Soars with Eagles

NOVEMBER 28

"A small boy whirls in circles, his arms outstretched ready to embrace all that surrounds him, giggling with wild abandon. The faster he turns the louder he laughs. His view of the world he knows is blurred and distorted. Nothing looks the way he remembers it. You know what? He doesn't care. His genuine joy continues to grow and fill the air. He is living in the absolute present, his senses heightened, and fully aware of all that he feels. When he finally collapses in an exhausted, yet satisfied, heap—all the while laughing between gasps and pants—*you* predictably ask, 'Why did you do that?' The boy replies, minus the sad confusion of your inquiry, 'Because it's fun!' What better reason could be given? Take the time today to rediscover what makes your world spin!"

— Joseph & Dondi

Dailies _____

NOVEMBER 29

"From what depth does your inability to trust take root? What is obstructing its route? You cannot force it to break-free of the rock and sod. You must instinctively, like nature, continue to strive for the light knowing—trusting—it has been right there all the while."

— *Christopher*

November 30

"The raindrop is not concerned about where it falls. It is a single, yet vital, particle of a far larger collective. It works with countless more to nourish our Mother Earth. Be like the solitary drop of rain—work and strive for the greater good and you will flourish!"

– *The One Who Soars with Eagles* **365**

December 1

"As your insight expands to a more panoramic view, you will be more accepting of multiple landscapes seen. You will realize your vision, once thought limited, is, in reality, unlimited. The terrain and the heavens spread before you reveal approaching storms and wondrous serenity. This spectacular view atop the highest perch comes in the faithful acceptance that what is will be, and that is how it has always been."

– The One Who Soars with Eagles

366

DECEMBER 2

"You soar with the Great Spirit forever—your sight should be equally infinite."

— The One Who Soars with Eagles

Dailies _____

DECEMBER 3

"You cannot speak what you do not know. If one is blind to the truth how can they be expected to live it? Shine your light on the truth so others may see."

— Robert

DECEMBER 4

"The course of the mighty river begins with the smallest trickle from the gentle stream. All great things begin with something seemingly small. All must be in order to become what is—all equally significant, steering toward one heavenly goal."

— The One Who Soars with Eagles **369**

Dailies _____

DECEMBER 5

"Fear can be helpful, fear can be a hindrance. It can help you live or it can prevent you from it. Do not cower in the darkness. Face each morn with wonder and grace for it has been given to each of us selflessly."

– Laura

DECEMBER 6

"If you do not know, ask. If you do not ask, do not act as if you did. It is knowledge, not assumptions, that advances you forward."

– Oliver

<u>371</u>

Dailies _____

DECEMBER 7

"Jacks can be played alone. But that don't mean it has to be, ya know? Share the game. It means more *with* more!"

— Dondi

December 8

"Just because the light has been turned on in the room does not guarantee the inhabitants have opened their eyes to see."

– Thomas

Dailies _____

DECEMBER 9

"There is no point seeking a new lease on life unless you realize it will not take effect until you knowingly and willingly sign it! Sign for your gift with a firm hand. Your intent and commitment are forever binding."

— Christopher

<u>374</u>

December 10

"Simple faith, no matter its origin, may not always clear the mist of the approaching storm. But it will allow you to accept what is and what will come once the clouds have parted."

— Robert

DECEMBER 11

"It is time to make up your bed. You sought the responsibility and the desire has been answered. It is at your door—shall you open it or will you cower in the far corner of the self-imposed "safety" that is nothing but a façade? Face life—live life—BE the life you sought. Be brave, my child, for all the strength and muscle you need is yours! Cannot find it? It resides, as all you need, within the truth of your heart. *Ask and ye shall receive'* is not a myth. Own it and own up to it."

— The Collective

December 12

"Disappointment can be nothing more than the opportunity to drive another route. Do you have it within yourself to turn onto the road less traversed? Or are you content whining in bumper-to-bumper traffic?"

– Thomas

Dailies _____

DECEMBER 13

"Look into your mind for knowledge. Look above your mind for truth. Look into your heart to discern the difference."

— Oliver

<u>378</u>

Day-To-Day Reminders _____

December 14

"Can you truthfully be angered if another does not follow your rules if you have never carved them in stone in the first place? In order to stand your own ground you, and only you, must first lay claim to it."

— Robert

DECEMBER 15

"When you 'speak your mind' are you truthfully articulating what is or how you choose to perceive it in the heat of the moment? Clear your line of sight in order to bring forth the light and allow it to douse your 'craving' to be right."

— Pamela

December 16

"The offense is not how it falls upon the ears of another but why you permitted it to roll from your tongue in the first place."

— Robert

381

DECEMBER 17

"The winds of change pick up the dried debris in order for new life to rise to the surface. If it no longer serves—habits, characteristics, patterns—then know to release it. Allow the wind to clear you, cleanse you, heal you and finally release you!"

— The One Who Soars with Eagles

DECEMBER 18

"Purity exists within you. But, from time to time, a squirt of Spiritual Windex sure wouldn't hurt. You need to see in order to be seen!"

– Thomas

<u>383</u>

DECEMBER 19

"Nurture your own seed from the beginning, carefully cultivating your path and direction as you grow. Getting tangled within your own roots prevents your own growth. Reach for the light, for the light is your reality of the highest order."

— Christopher

DECEMBER 20

"Fly with us, but soar for yourself!"

— The One Who Soars with Eagles

December 21

"The light is always there. Whether illuminating a new day dawning or radiating a beautiful sunset comforting you as you reflect upon the day now at your back. The light, I assure you, is always there. Perhaps you cannot see it at present. There are times when the obvious is not so. Understand and accept that this is fine. Do not worry—each of us can be 'too close' to a situation, 'too wrapped up' in a moment or outcome. This is all part of your physical incarnation. To deny yourself even the frustrations is denying yourself life. The key to it all is knowing—nay—believing the light is always there. Especially when you think you believe otherwise."

– The One Who Soars with Eagles

_____ *Dailies*

DECEMBER 22

"Give of yourself. Give to yourself. The benefit is mutual and ever-lasting. One not before the other but side-by-side, balanced equals within, throughout and above."

— *Laura*

<u>387</u>

_____ *Day-To-Day Reminders*

Dailies _____

DECEMBER 23

"A dog sitting, guarding, at your feet. A kitten curled peacefully, lovingly, in your lap. How can these physical manifestations of pure, unconditional love be void of a Soul, a Spirit? Love comes from the Creator in all ways. Do not permit an antiquated thought or ideal to deprive you of even one. Bless your animal brethren. Open yourself to all they teach from the most humblest and purest of hearts."

– *The One Who Soars with Eagles & Joseph*

Day-To-Day Reminders _____

December 24

"Your higher self is reaching to your inner self. Your inner self reaches for your higher self. The time you spend in meditation bridges the gap between the two. Do you recall Michelangelo's 'Creation of Adam?' The hand of God touching that of the hand of Man? That's all it takes: one touch. One touch will light up your inner world."

– Robert

DECEMBER 25

"A present is given from love. This gift goes from God to you in love and, through you, His love goes to others. It is an ongoing gift passed down through time and all ages will benefit from it. Hold on to it tightly as a child grasps a new toy on Christmas morn with love and wide-eyed wonderment of the magic within your hand."

— Robert

December 26

"The right-handed can write alongside the left-handed with ease and grace. This detente comes from merely switching places at the table. Take a moment to see things from the point of view from your so-called antagonist. Solutions to angst are often simple if you allow it to be so."

– Joseph

Dailies _____

DECEMBER 27

"Everyone is different, yet so many struggle to be 'like everybody else.' Rejoice in all diversity—especially your own—for there is no greater source of learning acceptance and all of its facets."

— Martin

December 28

"Emptiness cannot fill a hole. Replace envy for another with love and gratitude for yourself."

– Oliver

Dailies _____

DECEMBER 29

"We've all heard it. We've all said it. 'Bad things happen.' Almost like a mantra or an excuse. Well, you know what? Good things happen, too. There's a mantra for you! Try that one on for size and watch your world change!"

– Thomas

Day-To-Day Reminders _____

DECEMBER 30

"It proves pointless to fill your library with leather bound volumes when you do not intend to read them cover-to-cover. A life spent collecting for the sake of appearance is nothing more than a life spent. A tome well worn and dog-eared serves as a beautiful to behold reminder of both your lessons learned as well as those taught."

395

— Christopher

Dailies _____

DECEMBER 31

"You do not have to know the road before you walk it. You only need to know to take the steps. If you focus only on the planning of your journey you are sure to miss the incidentals along the way. Look left, look right, look above and beyond. What do you see? Why are you seeing it? It can make you wonder…and it should. Since nothing is merely chance then these "incidentals" are, by logical definition, pretty important after all, aren't they? Now how silly do you feel? Yea. I thought as much. Now open that door and step out into… well, you'll see…"

– *Thomas*

"Let us not look back in anger,
nor forward in fear,
but around us in awareness."

— James Thurber

www.ingramcontent.com/pod-product-compliance
Lightning Source LLC
Chambersburg PA
CBHW031611160426
43196CB00006B/96